P9-EDA-313

SPC TOOLS FOR EVERYONE

Also available from Quality Press

Statistical Quality Control Methods
Irving W. Burr

Statistical Process Control Methods: For Long and Short Runs
Gary K. Griffith

*The Self-Instructional Route to Statistical Process Control
and Just-in-Time Manufacturing*
I. Louis Bare and Bebe Bare

SPC for Practitioners: Special Cases and Continuous Processes
Gary Fellers, PhD

Quantitative Methods for Quality and Productivity Improvement
Marilyn K. Hart and Robert F. Hart

Statistical Process Control in Manufacturing
J. Bert Keats and Douglas C. Montgomery

Glossary and Tables for Statistical Control, Second Edition
ASQC Statistics Division

To request a complimentary catalog of publications, call 800-248-1946.

SPC TOOLS FOR EVERYONE

John T. Burr

ASQC Quality Press
Milwaukee, Wisconsin

Riverside Community College
Library
OCT '98   4800 Magnolia Avenue
Riverside, CA 92506

TS 156.8 .B87 1993

Burr, John T., 1932-

SPC tools for everyone

SPC Tools for Everyone
John T. Burr

Burr, John T.
    SPC tools for everyone / John T. Burr.
        p.   cm.
    Rev. ed. of: SPC tools for operators.
    Includes bibliographical references and index.
    ISBN 0–87389–244–5
        1. Process control—Statistical methods.   2. Quality control—
Statistical methods.   I. Burr, John T.   SPC tools for
operators.   II. Title.
    TS156.8.B87   1993
    670.42'01'15—dc20   93–9436
                                                        CIP

© 1993 by ASQC
All rights reserved. No part of this book may be reproduced in any form or by any means, electronic, mechanical, photocopying, recording, or otherwise, without the prior written permission of the publisher.

10 9 8 7 6 5 4 3

ISBN 0-87389-244-5

Acquisitions Editor: Susan Westergard
Production Editor: Annette Wall
Marketing Administrator: Mark Olson
Set in Goudy and Gill Sans by Montgomery Media, Inc.
Cover design by Montgomery Media, Inc.
Printed and bound by BookCrafters, Inc.

ASQC Mission: To facilitate continuous improvement and increase customer satisfaction by identifying, communicating and promoting the use of quality principles, concepts, and technologies; and thereby be recognized throughout the world as the leading authority on, and champion for, quality.

For a free copy of the ASQC Quality Press Publications Catalog, including ASQC membership information, call 800-248-1946.

Printed in the United States of America

  Printed on acid-free recycled paper

 ASQC
Quality Press
611 East Wisconsin Avenue
Milwaukee, Wisconsin 53202

CONTENTS

• •

FOREWORD

The industrial revolution brought about a new way of life to people engaged in the manufacture of interchangeable parts. This required workers in plants to think in a new way, different from what had been the norm for prior years. In place of individual mating of handcrafted parts came the requirement for large masses of similar parts meeting specifications. It was necessary for inspectors to check on the acceptability of parts and assemblies and to remove from the "line" those that did not conform to requirements. The rejected ones were either reworked or set aside as scrap, adding to the cost of the product.

Today's industrial world, with international competition, is in a constant battle for "fair share" of the marketplace, and customers are looking for value as well as the desired goods. Value is the quality/cost ratio of the product or service for sale. Today, companies must increase the quality of their products and, at the same time, must reduce the cost of providing them.

Bringing about increased value to products or service requires a cultural change in thinking for everyone in today's work force. This new way of thinking requires changes in attitudes of workers and management alike. In addition to the managerial revolution that is taking place, where management becomes team members with workers at all levels, there must come an understanding of basic tools to handle and control variation that comes with mass production. Workers must form new attitudes that will lead to 100 percent conformance to realistic specifications as a normal way of doing the job.

Just as all schoolchildren are taught the basics of arithmetic, so must all in the work force be taught the basics of process quality control. There always will be a need for advanced courses in both, but the basics must become an accepted way of life and a foundation for building greater understanding as more work experience and training in advanced quality tools are acquired with time.

Albert D. Rickmers

PREFACE

As I began teaching statistical process control in companies around the United States, I found that there was apparently no basic, nonstatistical book to introduce SPC to nontechnical people. Since 1978, I have been on the Publications Management Board of the American Society for Quality Control. Most of that time I was either the chair of the Technical Media Committee or vice president of Publication Services. In these capacities, I have reviewed nearly all of the new book projects of the Society. In all that time, most of the books that I saw were written by quality engineers for their peers in the company, i.e., they were heavily statistical rather than descriptive.

I set out to create a workbook for use in introducing operators, technicians, clerks, and secretaries to the mysteries of SPC. This book intends to provide the student with easily understood definitions of terms and statistical concepts. I have successfully used these materials teaching all levels of personnel in a number of companies over the past seven years.

I am greatly in debt to Albert D. Rickmers, who was certainly one of the best teachers in the field, for an overall approach to the subject. His goal has always been that of KISS, "Keep It Statistically Simple." He also has demonstrated that SPC can be fun as well as being vital to the health of both manufacturing and service industries in the United States.

INTRODUCTION

This book describes the use of tools for statistical process control (SPC). Most of these tools are not statistical, but are pictures of information. Whoever said that "a picture is worth a thousand words" knew what he or she was talking about. Pictures of information make it easier to talk to others about your ideas, data, or decisions. Pictures of information let everyone in a group see the same things at the same time.

Why do we need SPC? If your company, division, or unit is to continue providing jobs, you will need to use SPC. Survival of the company will depend on SPC because competitors who use SPC will be able to make product or provide services better and faster. But your company can do the same and do it better. Your company will not only survive but it will grow.

SPC is similar to making toast. When you get up in the morning, you put bread into the toaster. You press down on the lever and the toasted bread pops up. If the toast is burnt, you can scrape the black off and eat the result. This makes the toast edible, but what will happen the next time you make toast? Of course, it will burn too. And the next, and the next. This is product control. Some people do not like to use the words *product control*. They would prefer *product disposition* or some other name.

Product control sorts out the bad product from the good product so that the good product can be sold and the bad product can be reworked or thrown away. Many companies are controlling product quality this way.

For the process of toasting bread, you can do something about the process. You can change the setting on the side of the toaster to make lighter toast the next time. This is your other choice when the toast burns. This is *process control*. You changed the process because the product was not what you wanted. You can do the same thing with your machine, manufacturing line, information system, office system, purchasing system, or any other operation in the plant or office.

Sometimes management will not let us make the changes that we know need to be made. However, American managers are beginning to learn that process control is important for the survival of the company. You can help them by using the tools in this book to show them why you need to use process control. You also can help by showing when changes need to be made.

There are 14 tools described in this book. These are listed below. Let's look at how they work together.

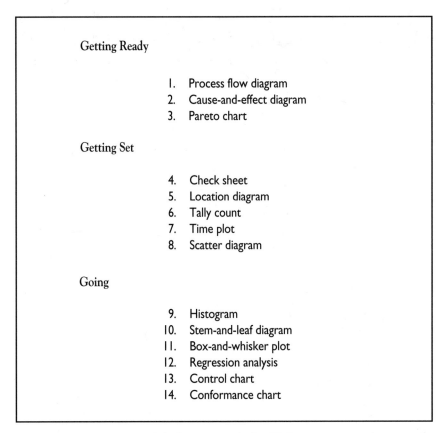

Getting Ready

   1. Process flow diagram
   2. Cause-and-effect diagram
   3. Pareto chart

Getting Set

   4. Check sheet
   5. Location diagram
   6. Tally count
   7. Time plot
   8. Scatter diagram

Going

   9. Histogram
  10. Stem-and-leaf diagram
  11. Box-and-whisker plot
  12. Regression analysis
  13. Control chart
  14. Conformance chart

Fabulous 14 tools for SPC.

The first three tools are the most important. We must understand the process in order to control it. In the toaster example, if we did not know what the control knob is for, we could not change the setting. Making a picture of the process helps us to understand what is happening and how it happens. Making a picture of the causes of problems helps us to know why things happen to our process or product. Making a picture of the number of times things occur helps us to identify the important things to work on. We will discuss each in detail.

The next five tools are the picturing of data on the product, process, or system without the use of statistics. Sometimes these are the only methods used for looking at information.

The last six tools are those that use statistics. Statistics are just numbers, and we can all work with numbers. We have been doing it all our lives—at the store, at work, and at home. The last six tools also are pictures, just like the ones we have talked about already. We have added some lines, points, or numbers to them. These will help you and your manager make good decisions about your process.

1
GETTING READY

BRAINSTORMING

Brainstorming is one method of obtaining ideas from a group of people. It has rules that must be followed. Brainstorming can be used to get the ideas of the group organized into a process flow diagram or a cause-and-effect diagram. Flow diagrams and cause-and-effect diagrams are explained in the two following sections.

The rules of brainstorming are easy.

1. Clearly define the goal of the brainstorming session. This is very important. You do not want people working on two different problems.

2. Try to have all people give their ideas in three words or less.

3. Write down all ideas. Some may seem silly, but they may lead to an idea that could help solve the problem.

4. Do not judge any idea. If someone laughs or says that it cannot be done, tell the group members that they are there to get all ideas out. Write it down.

5. Make the ideas visible so that everyone can see them easily.

6. Put the ideas down on paper so they can be copied later. Do not use a blackboard because someone will have to copy the ideas before the group leaves the room. If you have an overhead projector, you can list the ideas on a transparency.

PROCESS FLOW DIAGRAMS

As explained in the introduction, we need to know how a process works before we can control it. In the factory, we need to know how raw materials come to the machine. We need to know in what order the machine uses the raw materials to make the product. We need to know where in the process the tests are made. We need to know where the product goes when we have made it. All of these things can be pictured in a flow diagram. For example, let us try one for toasting bread (Figure 1.1).

The raw material is the bread. Is it fresh from the bakery? If so, it will take longer to get brown. If it is old and dry, it may burn at the same setting. Or was it frozen?

The machine is the toaster, of course. The operation is simple, but where do you set the knob for the first piece? In the middle? Wherever you do set it, you probably will check the bread prior to the completion of the operation. The test may only be to watch for smoke or it may be that you become tired of waiting for the toast to pop up and do it manually. Either way you have made an in-process test.

The product is the toast. Will you butter it and eat it? Or will you add jelly and peanut butter? In the second case you might not be so concerned with how dark the toast is.

This is perhaps a trivial example, but all the parts of the process flow diagram are here. These same parts will work for any process. It will work for a complicated screw machine, an injection molding device, an assembly operation, or any other factory operation. It also will work for staff processes, such as purchasing methods, design systems, secretarial functions, or office operations.

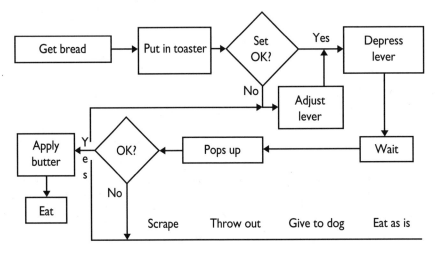

Figure 1.1
Process flow diagram for toasting bread.

HOW TO MAKE A PROCESS FLOW DIAGRAM

The first thing to do is to gather together everyone who knows about the process. Be sure that you have lots of chart paper, felt-tip pens, and masking tape. Together, start the picture at the beginning. What is the first thing that happens? What is the next thing that happens? This continues throughout the entire process.

At times during the process of making a diagram, you may need to ask additional questions, such as the following:

- Where does the (material) come from?
- How does the (material) get to the process?
- Who makes the decision (if one is needed)?
- What happens if the decision is "yes" or "no"?
- Is there anything else that has to be done at this point?
- Where does the product of this operation go?
- What tests are performed on the product at each part of the process?
- What tests are performed on the process?
- What happens if the test is out of tolerance?

There are many other questions that could be used. Usually it is not a good idea to ask the question, "Why?" This question may make one of the team members angry. However, you may want to ask that question if you think the team needs to know.

There are many ways to put the information onto a chart. It is the information, not the form, that is important. The easiest way is to use boxes and lines as we did in the toaster example. It can be helpful to use the diamond symbol for a decision because it is easy to draw two lines out of the corners. Figures 1.2 and 1.3 show two examples of flow diagrams.

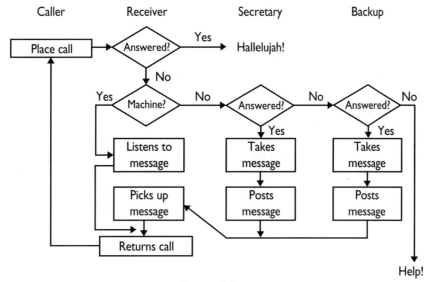

Figure 1.2
Process flow diagram for telephone tag.

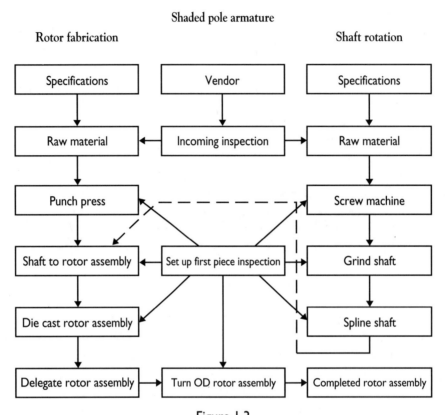

Figure 1.3
Process flow diagram of an assembly operation
showing the inspection points.

Now you have a picture of the process and everyone else sees the same picture. This picture can be used to decide what to do to improve the process, what might be done to solve a problem, or to train new personnel in using the process.

SUMMARY
- Before trying to solve a problem, define it.
- Before trying to control a process, understand it.
- Before trying to control everything, find out what is important.
- Start by picturing the process.

CAUSE-AND-EFFECT DIAGRAMS

The cause-and-effect diagram is a method of organizing information about a problem or a goal. It is a good way to picture what people think are the causes of a problem or what to do to achieve a goal.

The process is easy. Start with a clear definition of the problem or goal. Does everyone understand it? Put this in a box on the right side of the chart paper. Draw a line to the left and put diagonal arrows as shown in Figure 1.4.

Label the arrows using the "four Ms and the P"—material, machine, measurement, method, and people. Other labels can be used if you want (Figure 1.5).

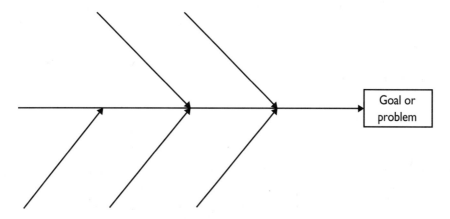

Figure 1.4
Basic structure of a cause-and-effect diagram.

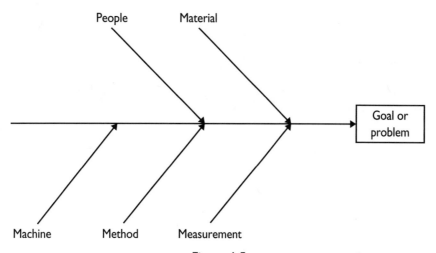

Figure 1.5
Generic cause-and-effect diagram with typical labels.

Now you or the team can begin to fill in the things that you think will cause the problem or help to achieve the goal (Figure 1.6). *NOTE:* The labels of the arrows have been changed.

This can be done alone or with a team. You will get more information if it is done with a team.

There are several items to remember in making cause-and-effect diagrams:

1. Write down everything people suggest. Do not judge.

2. The information rather than the form is important.

3. Where causes are put in the diagram is not important at first. They can go under any of the headings: materials, people, methods, etc.

4. The same cause can be in different places on the diagram if people want it that way.

5. Is it important for *all* persons to help in adding causes to the diagram.

6. If the diagram is not finished at the end of the meeting, you or others can add to it later.

7. Some companies post cause-and-effect diagrams so that their employees can add to them.

Figures 1.7 and 1.8 show two examples of diagrams that have been created by individuals or groups. Figure 1.7 shows some of the reasons or causes of nonproductive meetings. Sometimes it is easier for a group to work on how to make things bad. We know how to do that, and it's fun! Now we have to figure out how to do things better using the data in the diagram. Figure 1.8 shows how one company identified the possible causes of what it called "defects."

Over a few hours, any group can create a very large cause-and-effect diagram. Keep the time limit short: In 15 to 30 minutes, any group should be able to list most of the important causes. Stop when the ideas slow down.

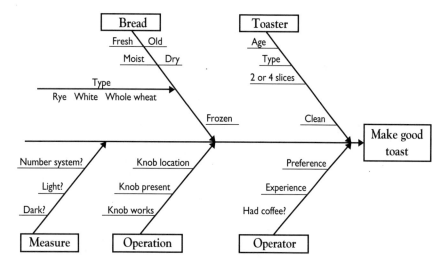

Figure 1.6
Cause-and-effect diagram for the process of making toast.

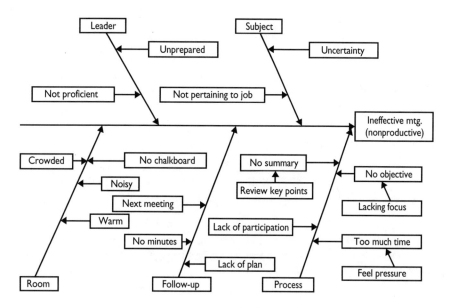

Figure 1.7
Cause-and-effect diagram for the causes of an ineffective meeting.

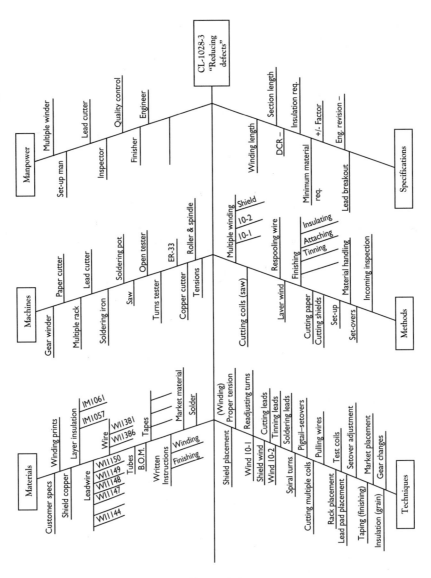

Figure 1.8
Cause-and-effect diagram for reducing defects in an
electrical equipment manufacturing process.

PARETO CHARTS

The Pareto chart is based on the Pareto principle. This principle was named for an Italian who, in the late 1800s, found that most of the wealth in Italy was owned by a few of the people. Today we find the same thing happening in the plant and the office. Most of our problems can be traced to a few causes.

Figure 1.9 shows one of several Pareto models. Figure 1.10 shows an every-member canvass of a church. The vertical axis is the amount pledged in dollars; the horizontal axis is the number of people who pledged that amount.

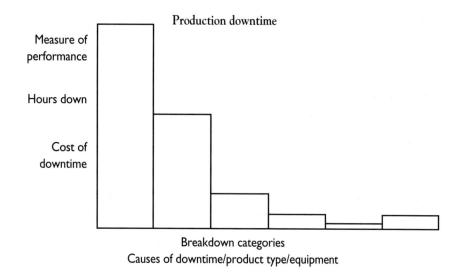

Figure 1.9
Generic Pareto chart.

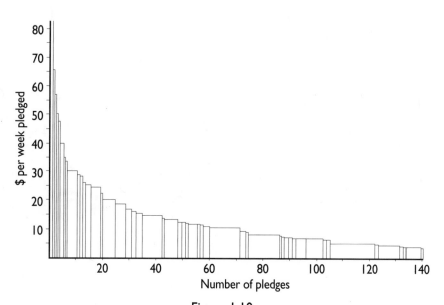

Figure 1.10
Pareto chart of the weekly pledges made by members for the support of
a church in Rochester, New York.

The 80/20 rule states that 80 percent of the problems come from 20 percent of the causes. The usual way to show this is with a bar chart. The height of each bar represents the number of times that cause happens. The causes are placed in order from the highest to the lowest. Figures 1.11 and 1.12 show two examples of the Pareto chart in action.

In the figures, it is clear what needs to be worked on first. For example, if we want to improve the quality of the strut rods, we first need to get rid of the handling damage and then work on grinder grit and white spots (Figure 1.11).

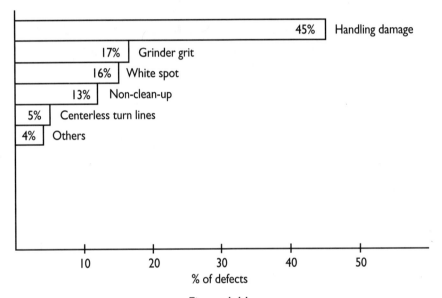

Figure 1.11
Pareto chart of the causes for nonconformities found on a strut rod.

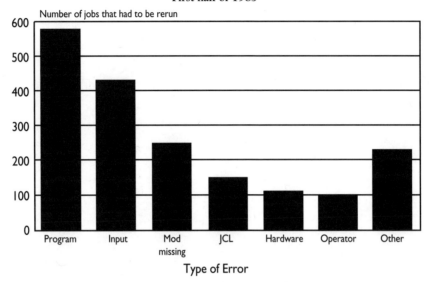

Figure 1.12
Pareto chart for the causes of jobs rerun in an information systems office.

2

IDENTIFYING WHAT TO MEASURE

· ·

Measurement is the basis of the quality process. To do SPC, we must measure something. We must collect data and information. Usually this is easy to see in manufacturing.

Recently, a young foreman walked into a training class shaking his head. When asked why, he said that he had a problem, but nothing to measure. We spent 20 minutes of class time making a process flow diagram and a cause-and-effect diagram. On these diagrams we wrote down 18 measurements that were already being made or that could be made. The foreman shook his head and said that now there were too many things to measure. In four minutes the class voted on the three most important measurements. The problem was solved in 24 minutes.

Understand the process using flow diagrams, cause-and-effect diagrams, and Pareto analysis. Find and write out the problems in the process. Ask the following questions:

- What do we measure?
- What could we measure?
- What should we measure?
- What can we measure?

Develop possible measures by brainstorming. Cause-and-effect diagrams also can be used here.

TYPES OF MEASUREMENT TECHNIQUES— NONMANUFACTURING APPLICATIONS

It is not easy to find something to measure when we are working in an office or performing a service for others. It will take everybody's imagination to develop good measures of quality.

1. *Rating systems*—Supplier rating systems, process audits, product audits, peer evaluations, market surveys, and customer surveys.

CAUTION: Seek expert help in devising the questionnaire or you may get the responses that you expect or that the respondent thinks you want. Remember the Edsel!

NOTE: These can be obtained immediately upon completion of the project and at a later date (e.g., six months) to assess long-term effectiveness of the projected components.

2. *Counting systems*—Anything that can be counted can be tracked, such as the following:
- Number of problems per delivery of a product
- Number of times a client tries before reaching you
- Number of problems by type of problem
- Number of tasks or subprocesses completed on time

3. *Measures*—Anything that can be measured can be tracked, such as the following:
- Time/days early/late delivery of product or task
- Time to reach person—wait or dead time
- Uptime or downtime of system—hard or soft
- Cycle time of the system or talks
- Productivity measures—hours/task
- Quality measures—fraction of goal achieved
- Cost of delivery—over/under

4. *Profiles and weighted profiles*—A profile is the summary of ratings given by survey participants to a set of product characteristics. These numbers can be added together to give a single number. If some characteristics are more important than others, they can be weighted. Weighting can be done by multiplying the rating by a number. If one characteristic is twice the value of another, the weighting number would be two. This is done to obtain a single measure from more than one characteristic of a project or task.

5. *Value analysis*—Value as defined by the customer plotted against the time used to obtain that portion of the needs.

CAUTION: Identify dependencies among the efforts. The customer may place low value on an activity that is vital to achieving something later that is of high value to the client. You may want to include the former as part of the latter.

6. *Minimizing the variability of the process*—as measured by the process capability index. (See the section on process capability.)

7. *Degree of centering of the process on nominal*—as measured by the deviation from nominal as a fraction of the process variability. For further information on these, refer to the discussions on specifications, histograms, and process capability.

Use these measures for self-improvement and to demonstrate progress. Do not use these measures to judge individual performance, especially between teams, projects, or individuals. Remember that it is the system that often affects performance. Office and plant personnel cannot change the system—only management can.

. . . .

THE IMPORTANCE OF THE SAMPLE

If the sample is not good, the plots and decisions made from the samples will not be good! What makes a sample good or bad?

1. The sample must represent the population. It should have close to the same average, spread, and shape as the population from which it is taken.

- You can take a *random* sample. Each item in the population has an equal chance of being chosen in the sample.
- You can take a *systematic* sample every so often or every x number of pieces from a continuous process.
- You can take a *stratified* sample. This is taking a part of the sample from each level of a box or each section of an area.

2. The sample must be large enough to answer your questions about the population.

- You will need a sample of more than 30 if you want to know the average and the standard deviation of the population.
- You will need more than 12 samples of four to five each if you want to know if the average or the variability of the population changes.
- You will need to take samples of more than 100 to estimate an attribute. (See Attributes, page 54.)
- The more data we have, the more we know about the population.

3
GETTING SET

CHECK SHEETS

The most common use of a check sheet is in the cockpit of an airplane. Before every flight, the captain and the crew go through a list and check off each item. This list includes all of the items that must be in working order to ensure a safe flight, such as fuel, oil pressure, warning lights, hydraulic pressures, flap indicator signals, and instrument operations. If the check sheet is not used, something might be forgotten. This could lead to a serious or fatal accident during takeoff or landing.

In some manufacturing processes, check sheets may be required to ensure safety or quality just as in an airplane. One example is shown in Figure 3.1. Another example of the use of check sheets is in training new personnel. This

Markings—identification
☐ ID tags on pallet
☐ Labels on each box
☐ Purchase order on pallet
☐ Quantities match

Banding
☐ Pallet banded four ways
☐ Edge protectors present

Packaging
☐ Top boxes level
☐ Boxes completely covered

Figure 3.1
Abbreviated check sheet for a warehouse operation.

is done to ensure that the new person has all the information needed to do the job. In offices, a check sheet is something used to record phone conversations with customers or clients. This check sheet is usually in the form of a series of questions. Quality assessments or evaluations are also done using check sheets (Figure 3.2). These are used so that an essential point will not be missed.

NOTE: Tally sheets and location sheets also can be considered as check sheets.

LOCATION DIAGRAMS

Location diagrams are pictures or drawings of the unit that is manufactured. On these diagrams the location of problems, defects, or nonconformities are marked. Two examples are shown in Figure 3.3 and 3.4. In Figure 3.3, we are looking at the number of cold solder joints on a printed circuit board. Note that the drawing need not be exact. It represents the part under study. The number of occurrences are put on the diagram using Xs or some other symbol. Location diagrams also can be used in staff processes to locate bottlenecks in the work flow process. In this case an office layout often is used as a location diagram. The traffic pattern, mail flow, typing in-baskets, or personnel are located on the diagram along with the problems encountered. In Figure 3.4, the two typing clerks closest to the door are receiving most of the typing jobs.

TALLY COUNTS

Tally counts are ordered counts of occurrences as illustrated in the location diagram. This time, however, they are in numerical order and usually made on data that are measured. They also can be used on counted data. If we were to measure the darkness of the toast we made over a month's time, we could put the results in tally count. Let us say that untoasted bread is a 1 and burnt toast is a 9. In between these we have a measurement device that gives us a whole number which is the darkness of the toast. A tally count like the one in Figure 3.5 could result.

Because of all the causes that we identified in the cause-and-effect diagram, we do not always get the same color of toast. That is the natural *variability* of the process of the operator, material, machine, method, and measurement. The tally count is a picture of this variability.

The center point of the tally count is the *median*. Half of the pieces of toast are above this value and half are below. In this case the median is 5. The value that has the most pieces of toast in it is called the *mode*. It also is 5.

☐ Quality policy is documented
☐ Quality assurance procedures are complete
☐ Quality measures are established and tracked
☐ Quality is regularly discussed with work force
☐ Quality is highest priority
☐ Training program is formal
☐ Proficiency is documented and certified
☐ Improvement programs are showing progress

Figure 3.2
Abbreviated check sheet for a quality system audit.

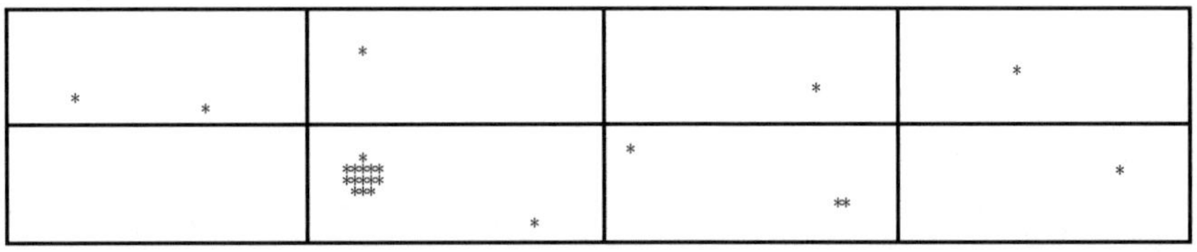

Figure 3.3
Location diagram for cold solder joints found on printed circuit
boards manufactured over several weeks.

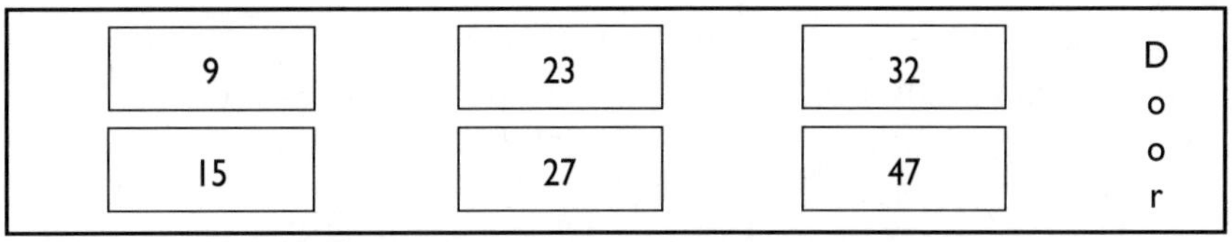

| 9 | 23 | 32 | D |
| 15 | 27 | 47 | o o r |

Average daily backlog over two-month period—
all positions have equal responsibility

Figure 3.4
Location diagram for backlogs in clerks' in-baskets.

Data	Tally diagram
6 , 5 , 3 , 5 , 7	1 I
4 , 4 , 5 , 5 , 3	2
5 , 6 , 4 , 5 , 4	3 X X X X
4 , 3 , 4 , 5 , 5	4 X X X X X X X X X X
7 , 6 , 5 , 6 , 5	5 X X X X X X X X X X X X
5 , 4 , 8 , 6 , 5	6 X X X X X X X X
3 , 7 , 6 , 7 , 4	7 X X X X X
7 , 6 , 4 , 6 , 4	8 X
	9

Figure 3.5
Example of a tally count made on the color of toast using
the chip distribution.

If we add up all the numbers of the pieces of toast, we get 203. We have 40 pieces of toast. The *average* piece of toast is 203 divided by 40. There is no average piece of toast, that is a single piece having a color of 5.1, just as there is no perfectly average person. But the average represents this *sample* of 40 pieces of toast.

The width of the measurement or sample is the highest number minus the lowest. This is the *range*, which is a measure of the variability of the sample. The range of the toast data is 8 minus 3, which is 5.

. . . .

TIME PLOTS

When data are taken in order over a period of time, the change of the measure with time may be seen. The data are plotted in the order that they were taken. In the case of the toast, it is by day. The result of this is called a time plot or trend chart (Figure 3.6).

If we wish to see what is happening more clearly, we can draw in the line that represents the average of the data. In this case the line is drawn at 5.1.

There are several other patterns that can be seen in time plots (Figures 3.7, 3.8, and 3.9). These patterns follow and are *trends* up (or down), *cycles*, and *alternating* values. The cycles might come from temperature changes by

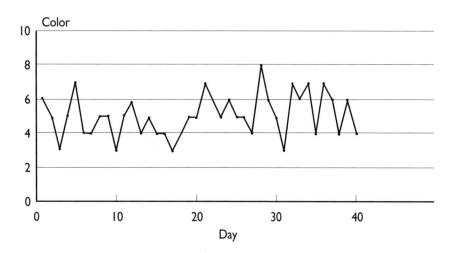

Figure 3.6
Example of a time plot of the color of the toast generated using
the chip distribution.

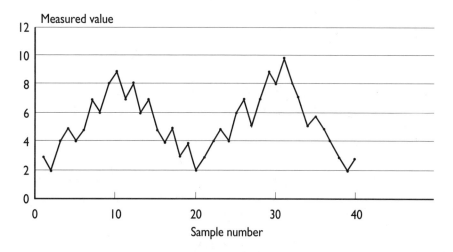

Figure 3.7
Example of a cycle appearing in a time plot.

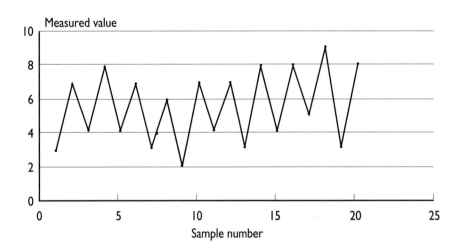

Figure 3.8
Example of alternating data appearing in a time plot.

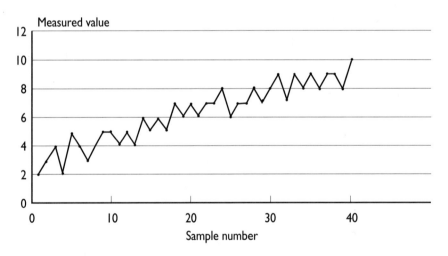

Figure 3.9
Example of an upward trend appearing in a time plot.

season or time of day. Cycles also might come during filling operations. Alternating values might come from measurements taken on different shifts or by different operators.

The important thing is to look at the time plot and determine what it is trying to tell you about the process by the patterns that you see, if there are any.

· ·

SCATTER DIAGRAMS

When you have two measurements on the same unit, you can look at the data using a scatter diagram. You can put the values for one measurement on the vertical line and the values for the other measurement on the horizontal line. Fill in the values between the range of values and plot the data on the diagram (Figure 3.10). In the case of the bread that we used to make toast, we know how old the bread was. We can plot this on the vertical axis. The darkness of the toast is plotted on the horizontal axis.

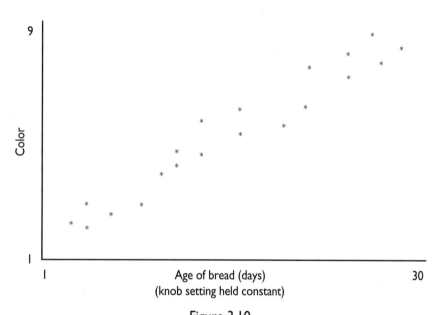

Figure 3.10
Scatter diagram of the relationship of the color of toast to the age of the bread. Generated using the chip distribution.

This is a useful chart for looking at products when two measurements are taken. In the first case, there is no relationship between the two measurements (Figure 3.11). In the second case, there seems to be a relationship but the process is variable (Figure 3.12). In the third case, the relationship is clear (Figure 3.13).

As in time plots, it is important to plot the data and then let the data tell you what is happening. One way is to draw two lines, one for the average of the vertical data and one for the horizontal data. This divides the plot into four quarters. If there are more data in two opposite quarters than in the other two opposite quarters, there is likely to be a relationship between the two measurements.

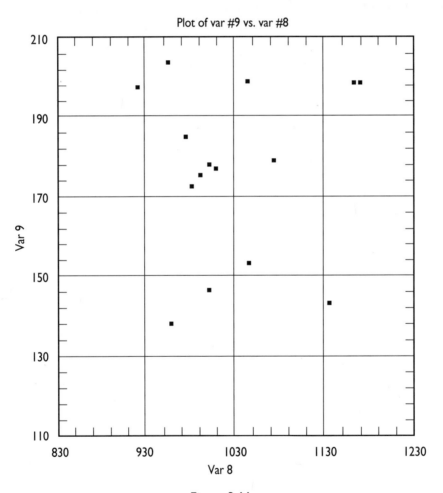

Figure 3.11

Example of a scatter diagram between variable numbers 8 and 9 of a recent experiment on plastic sheeting.

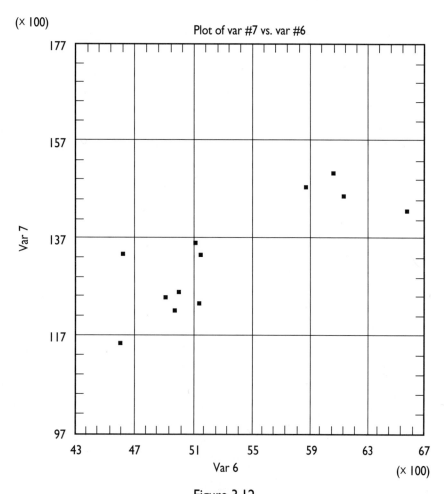

(× 100)

Plot of var #7 vs. var #6

Var 7

Var 6

(× 100)

Figure 3.12

Example of a scatter diagram between variable numbers 7 and 6
of a recent experiment on plastic sheeting.

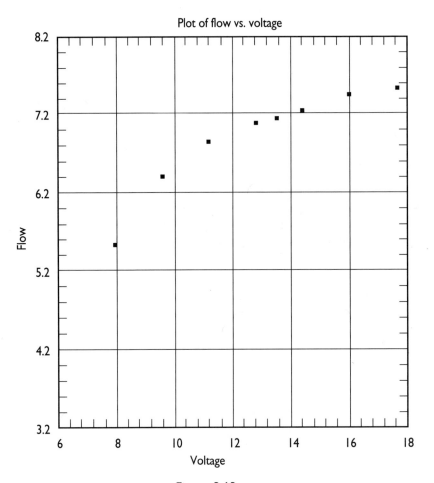

Figure 3.13
Example of a scatter diagram between the flow rate of a liquid
and the voltage applied to a valve.

4
GOING

· ·

HISTOGRAMS

A histogram is a tally count with boxes around the counts. These boxes are made so that they are as high as the number of Xs for that value in the tally count. This is done because we do not always make our Xs the same size or use the same spaces between each X. Making the right sized boxes gives a better picture of the shape of the sample variability. Figure 4.1 shows a histogram of the data on the color of toast.

Most data are high in the middle and trail out at each side. Often this is close to the same shape on both sides and is said to be *symmetrical*. Figure 4.1 is an example of this shape. This shape is also called *normal* because it is so often seen in the variability of natural processes and many measurement systems.

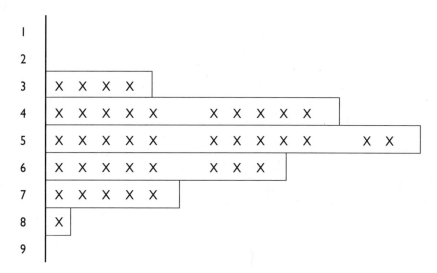

Figure 4.1
Tally count of Figure 3.5 made into a histogram.

By connecting the tops of the histogram, we can get a better picture of the shape of the sample variability. This is called the *distribution* of the sample.

By making a smooth curve over the histogram, we can get an idea of what all the samples might look like. This is called the distribution of the *population* of the measurement. It is shown for a skewed distribution in Figure 4.2. It is skewed to the right.

NOTE: Figure 4.2 is a *bar graph*, not a histogram. The sides of the bars are not against each other.

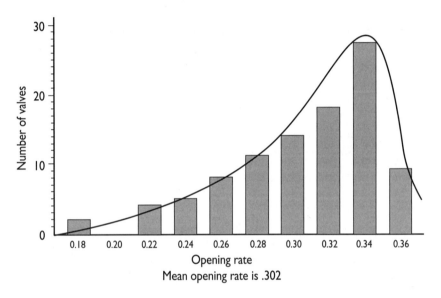

Mean opening rate is .302

Figure 4.2
Bar graph of the mean opening rate of a valve. The smooth line shows the shape of the distribution of all opening rates.

Note that histograms and samples do not always have only one peak. They may have two peaks or modes. These are called *bimodal*. Figure 4.3 is an example. There often is a cause for this. For example, the sleeves may be made on different machines or on different shifts.

There are many other shapes, but one that is seen often is the one that is stretched out to the left or right. This is called a *skewed* shape and can be skewed left or right.

In Figure 4.3 we have *class limits*. The class limits are the highest and lowest values that go into that group or class. There are two numbers that are from 0.3925 and 0.3929. They could be any one of the numbers 0.3925, 0.3926, 0.3927, 0.3928, or 0.3929. We do not know what they are unless we can look at the original data.

Class limits	Histogram	Frequency
0.3925–0.3929	XX	2
0.3920–0.3924	XXX	3
0.3915–0.3919	XXXXX	6
0.3910–0.3914	XXXXXXXXXXXX	12
0.3905–0.3909	XXXXXX	7
0.3900–0.3904	XXXXXXXXXX	10
0.3895–0.3899	XX	2
0.3890–0.3894	XX	2

Figure 4.3
Histogram of the sleeve diameters of a spindle.

It is important to examine the histogram. Look at its shape. A bimodal shape may tell you that there are two processes making the part, not one process. Look at its position or average compared to nominal. Is it close? Maybe the process needs to be adjusted. Look at its width or range. Is it wider than the tolerances? Maybe the process needs to be improved or made less variable.

NOTE: If your histogram is skewed, bimodal, or appears unusual, you should seek help from a quality expert.

ADDITIONAL INFORMATION ABOUT HISTOGRAMS

Histograms give us information about the location, the width of the spread, and the shape of the sample. These are called *statistics* of the sample and usually include the mean, *standard deviation*, and skewness. The *range* uses only two numbers to describe the variability. The standard deviation uses all the numbers in the samples. It can be calculated by using a calculator that has a statistics function on it or by estimating the standard deviation by dividing the range by a number:

- If the sample size is 10 to 29 divide the range by 4.
- If the sample size is 30 to 79 divide the range by 5.
- If the sample size is 80 or more divide the range by 6.

There is a calculation for the standard deviation that can be used without a calculator. It requires a great deal of arithmetic to use, however, and it will not be shown here.

If we have 30 or more measurements or units in the sample, we can say that the sample represents the population. The mean and the standard deviation and the shape of the sample distribution represent those of the population. They are said to be *estimators* of the mean, standard deviation, and shape of the population. The more data we have, the better the estimate.

The histogram of the sample can be compared to the tolerances or specifications (Figure 4.4). If the entire histogram can fit easily between the tolerance limits, we say that it is *capable* of meeting the tolerances. *NOTE:* In the example in Figure 4.4, the process is not on aim as made. The product shrinks as it cools and will be on aim by the next day.

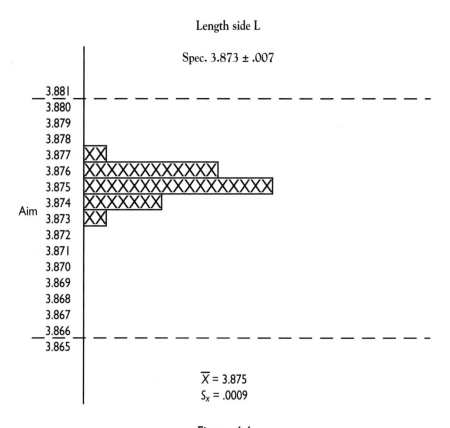

Length side L

Spec. 3.873 ± .007

$\overline{X} = 3.875$
$S_x = .0009$

Figure 4.4

Histogram of the length of plastic part stamped from a sheet. The tolerances are 3.873 ± 0.007 inch. The dimension will shrink 0.002 inch during the 24 hours following stamping.

HOW TO MAKE HISTOGRAMS

You have some data and you want to make a tally count and a histogram. The data might look like the following:

0.538, 0.537, 0.538, 0.540, 0.536, 0.539, 0.538, 0.541, 0.537
0.535, 0.540, 0.538, 0.539, 0.538, 0.537, 0.538, 0.542, 0.536

The first thing to do is look for the highest and lowest numbers. In this case these are 0.542 and 0.535. The range of the data is the difference between these numbers: 0.007.

The range should be divided into/from six to 15 groups or *classes*. These data have a range of 0.007 and we can make eight classes by having one class for each number in the data:

0.542
0.541
0.540
0.539
0.538
0.537
0.536
0.535

Now you place an X next to the number until all the data are in the table. To make a histogram enclose the Xs with a box of the right size.

Sometimes your data are more spread out than this example. The range is bigger:

0.538, 0.521, 0.542, 0.567, 0.555, 0.572, 0.533, 0.568, 0.553
0.579, 0.561, 0.547, 0.556, 0.567, 0.534, 0.545, 0.571, 0.550
0.562, 0.548, 0.553, 0.557, 0.564, 0.566, 0.555, 0.550, 0.568

The range is 0.579 minus 0.521, which equals 0.058.

To obtain the right number of classes, divide the range by 1, 2, 5, 10, 20, etc.

0.058 divided by .001 = 58
0.058 divided by .002 = 29
0.058 divided by .005 = 12
0.058 divided by .010 = 6

We can have 12 classes using a class interval of 0.005 for the example above. Always start the first cell with an interval that includes the smallest number in the data.

To make things easier for placing data in the table, start the first cell with 0.520. This is the lower class limit of the first class. The upper class limit of this class is 0.524. This class includes 0.520, 0.521, 0.522, 0.523, and 0.524. There are five numbers in the class and the class interval is 0.005.

This results in a table such as the following:

Class limits

0.575–0.579
0.570–0.574
0.565–0.569
0.560–0.564
0.555–0.559
0.550–0.554
0.545–0.549
0.540–0.544
0.535–0.539
0.530–0.534
0.525–0.529
0.520–0.524

The number that represents all the data in each class is called the *class mark*. It is the center value in the class limits. The class mark of the first class is 0.522; the class mark of the second class is 0.527. The class interval is the difference between the class marks of two classes next to each other. The class interval of the first class is 0.522 minus 0.527, which equals 0.005.

The use of class intervals of 0.003, 0.004, 0.006, 0.007, 0.008, or 0.009 is not incorrect. It would make it more difficult to put data into the table. Likewise, it would be harder to put data into the table if we started the first class with 0.521. It is harder to work with, but it is not wrong.

Computers almost always will use the range divided by the square root of the sample size for setting the class interval and will start the table on the smallest data point. This can result in some very strange class marks, class limits, and class intervals.

In the previous example, the class interval would be 0.058 divided by the square root of 27. This is equal to 0.0111621. The first class limits would be 0.5210000 to 0.5321621.

SUMMARY

• Determine the range of the data.

• Divide the range by 1, 2, 5, 10, 20, 50, 100, etc., to obtain a class interval that will give you from six to 15 classes.

• Start the first class at a logical place which includes the lowest data value.

. . . .

SPECIFICATIONS

Specifications are written documents. They tell us what to test, how to test it, and what the requirements are. The requirements usually are specified as *nominal* and *tolerance limits*. The tolerance limits are also called *specification limits*.

There are several forms for specifying the nominal and tolerance limits (# equals pounds):

- 102# ± 2#. Nominal is 102#; limits are 100 and 104#.
- 100 $^{-0}_{+4}$. Nominal is often 104#; limits are 100 and 104#.

This is not what customers really want. Customers usually mean that they do not want the product below 100#. If the product gets above 104# they will not be too concerned. Your company may set an *aim* or nominal that is different than 104#. What they set depends on the spread of the process and what will happen to the product if it is greater than 104. A 100# minimum means that no nominal is specified by the customer, but your company may specify an aim or nominal for the process. (Nominal is the value that the process average should be.)

Tolerance limits are those values within which all of the product must be. This is related to the spread of the data.

Specifications are defined by the customer or the user of the product. It always is best to include the supplier or the maker of the product in arriving at a set of specifications.

1. Specifications must be met *all* the time.

2. Processes must be held as close to nominal as possible.

Only by doing these two things can U.S. industries compete successfully on the world market. Our competitors are doing this, which is why their quality is better than ours and why their products work better and last longer than many of ours.

In some companies, product that does not meet the tolerances is released. This is regrettable, but there are times when this is done for the company's interest. We all have to understand that this must stop. However, we cannot stop it all at once. Everyone must work toward the day when it will no longer be necessary to release product that does not meet tolerances.

PROCESS CAPABILITY: SPECIAL APPLICATION OF HISTOGRAMS

Process capability is a method of comparing what the process is able to do in meeting tolerances. The process is the machines, operators, raw materials, tests, and methods used to make the product. We must find out if the process can make good quality product all the time. This is the capability of the process.

The process capability is obtained from a large sample of the process. The data are put into a computer. The average and the standard deviation are calculated by the computer for us.

The process capability is obtained by the following formula:

$$\frac{\text{Upper tolerance} - \text{Lower tolerance}}{6 \times \text{Standard deviation}}$$

Often this is called the process capability index (PCI) of the process.

A PCI of 1.0 means that the spread of data just fits inside the tolerances. A PCI of 1.3 is better. Ideally, the PCI should be larger than 2.0.

CAUTION: The PCI does not indicate where the process is. It only indicates that if the average is on nominal, the spread of the data will or will not stay inside the tolerances all the time.

The average of the process is compared to the nominal of the specification. If it is off nominal, the process should be adjusted back to nominal. That is why we need the average as well as the standard deviation for the process.

CAUTION: Before adjusting the average to nominal, check with your supervisor or quality assurance person. This is done to see if the process is enough off nominal to warrant a change (Figure 4.5).

Quality is necessary in today's competitive market. Our processes must always meet the specifications or tolerances. The process average should always be on or very close to the nominal and the variability must always be small enough to give us a PCI of larger than 1.3.

Method I: If the process is in control (see Chapter 1), the process capability can be obtained from the range chart.

Method II: For a new process, the process capability is estimated using the best operating conditions possible. The best operator, the best raw materials, and the best setup are used. When all the bugs are worked out of the process, take 40 pieces in a row. Have the computer calculate the average of the standard deviation and calculate the PCI. Compare this to what your company requires for a PCI of a new process.

If the process is not capable of meeting the requirements, something must be done. The following actions can be taken.

1. Review the specifications. *Do not* change them without consulting the customer. Change the specifications only if they can be changed without affecting the quality of the product.

2. Change or redesign the process. Often the operators can be helpful in locating problems and things that need to be improved.

3. Change or redesign the product.

4. Have another company make the product.

5. Stop production.

The last two solutions are not very good for keeping jobs in your company, but quality must be maintained. Processes that cannot meet specifications *all the time* lead to poor quality products.

ADDITIONAL INFORMATION ON PROCESS CAPABILITY: DEFINITIONS

(*NOTE:* These are not official ASQC definitions.)

1. *Process capability*—The *natural tolerance* of the process which is the average plus and minus three standard deviations.

2. *Process compatibility*—The ability or extent to which a process can meet realistic specifications under the best conditions and when the process is in statistical control.

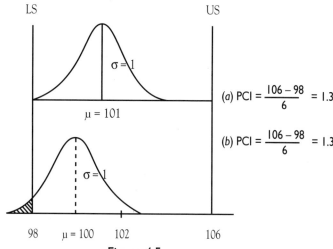

Figure 4.5

Distribution curves for two processess that have the same process capability index of 1.3.(*a*) The process is capable and is meeting the specifications; (*b*) the process is capable of meeting the specifications but is not doing it.

3. *Process capability index (PCI or C$_p$)*—The ratio of the width of the specification to the natural tolerance of the process. Many companies require that their suppliers have process capabilities of 1.3 or higher.

$$\frac{\text{Upper spec limit} - \text{Lower spec limit}}{6 \times \text{Standard deviation}}$$

4. *Process capability ratio (PCR)*—This is the reciprocal of the PCI. Many companies require a PCR of 0.75 or less.

$$\frac{6 \times \text{Standard deviation}}{\text{Upper spec limit} - \text{Lower spec limit}} = \frac{1}{\text{PCI}}$$

5. *C$_{pk}$*—The ratio between the process average minus the nearest specification limit and three standard deviations of the process. Most companies require a C$_{pk}$ of greater than 1.3.

$$\frac{\overline{X} - \text{Nearest spec limit}}{3 \times \text{Standard deviation}}$$

Some examples of different process capabilities are shown in Figure 4.6.

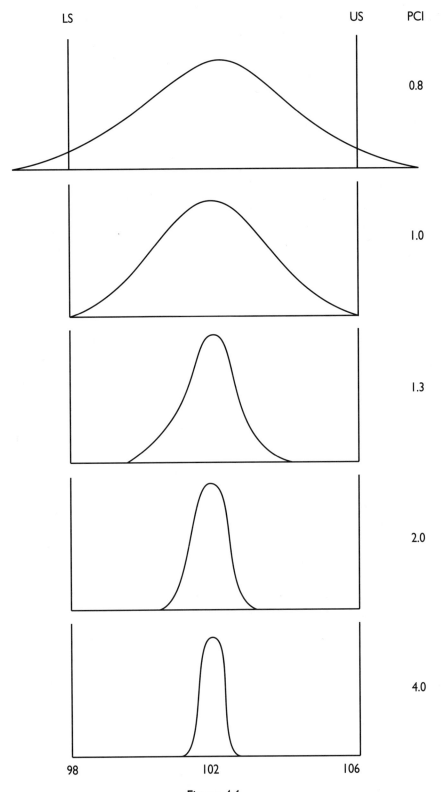

Figure 4.6
Distribution curves for different process capability indices.

• •

STEM-AND-LEAF DIAGRAMS

This is a special case of the histogram. In the measurement of sleeve diameters (Figure 4.3) the use of a histogram causes us to lose information. We do not know what the two values are between 0.3924 and 0.3929 in this histogram. We only know that there are two values, but we no longer know what they are.

One way to keep track of the data we put into a histogram is to use a stem-and-leaf diagram. This is done by locating the right pocket or *class* for the measurement. Then we put the last digit of the value into the histogram instead of an X. In Figure 4.7, the 7 of 0.3927 goes in the upper class 0.392^*. Likewise, the 4 of 0.3924 goes in the lower class of 0.392^+.

The first group of digits is the *stem* and the second is the *leaf*. Figure 4.8 shows another stem-and-leaf diagram.

Computers often will give you stem-and-leaf diagrams. They are studied and evaluated just like histograms. We need to look at (1) where they are centered, (2) width of the variability, and (3) shape of the distribution.

Stem	Leaf											Frequency
0.392^*	7	6										2
0.392^+	4	0	1									3
0.391^*	8	5	9	6	8	7						6
0.391^+	3	2	0	4	0	1	2	2	4	3	3	3 · 12
0.390^*	9	6	5	8	8	6	6					7
0.390^+	1	0	4	3	3	2	2	1	4	3		10
0.389^*	5	7										2
0.389^+	0	4										2

Figure 4.7
Stem-and-leaf diagram for the data
used to construct the histogram of Figure 4.3.

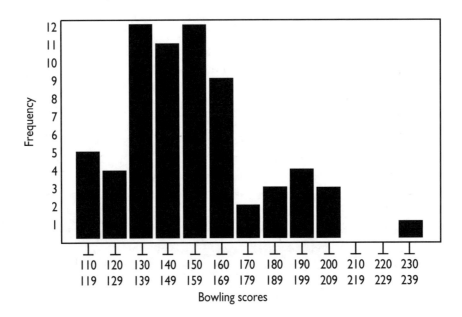

11 *	1 1 3 3 7	5
12 *	0 8 9 9	4
13 *	0 0 1 1 4 5 5 5 6 6 8 8	12
14 *	0 1 1 2 2 4 7 8 8 9 9	11
15 *	0 0 0 3 3 3 3 5 6 6 9 9	12
16 *	0 0 0 2 4 6 7 7 8	9
17 *	0 4	2
18 *	1 8 9	3
19 *	0 8 8 8	4
20 *	3 5 9	3
21 *		0
22 *		0
23 *	3	1

Figure 4.8
Histogram and stem-and-leaf diagram of the bowling scores
of a student at the Rochester Institute of Technology.

BOX-AND-WHISKER PLOTS

BOX-AND-WHISKER PLOTS
The box-and-whisker plot is a plot that computers will give you. You do not have to calculate anything for these. They are used to compare different samples from the same population. They also are used to compare samples from different populations.

The center line inside the box is the median of the sample (Figure 4.9). The median is the middle value when the data are put in numerical order (*ranked*).

The sides of the box contain the middle half of the numbers in the sample of the ranked data (Figure 4.10).

The end of each line (whisker) is the highest and lowest number in the sample (Figure 4.11).

Figure 4.12 shows an example of a box-and-whisker plot in action.

The spread is least on the second shift. The averages of the shifts are close to each other.

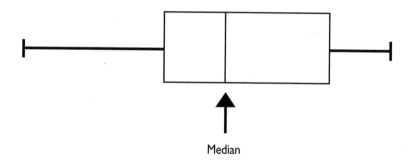

Figure 4.9
Box-and-whisker plot showing the position of the median.

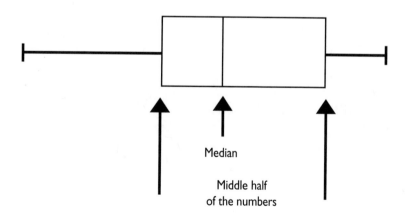

Figure 4.10
Box-and-whisker plot showing the position of the ends of the box.

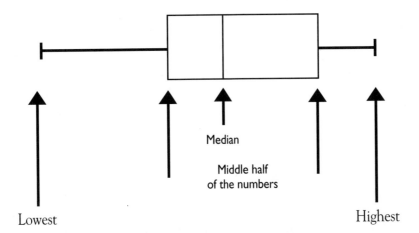

Figure 4.11
Box-and-whisker plot showing the position of the ends of the whiskers.

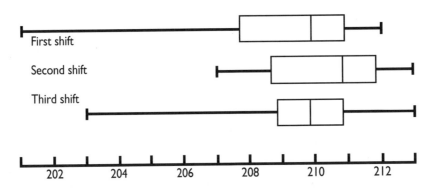

Figure 4.12
Example of a box-and-whisker diagram for data
on parts manufactured on three different shifts.

HOW TO MAKE BOX-AND-WHISKER PLOTS

It usually is easier to make box-and-whisker plots when there is an odd number of data points in the sample. This can be 5, 7, 9, 11, or more pieces of data in the sample. The more data in the sample, the better; however, there should be fewer than 30.

Arrange the data in order from the lowest to the highest (Figure 4.13). This is called ranking the data.

Find the middle number. This is the *median*. If there is an even number in the sample, the median is halfway between the two middle values. In this case it is 101. It usually has a symbol of M (Figure 4.14).

Data in the sample

101, 98, 104, 102, 100, 100, 105, 102, 101

Ordered data

Number	1	2	3	4	5	6	7	8	9
Value	98	100	100	101	101	102	102	104	105

Figure 4.13
Data as taken and ranked in order for use in
making a box-and-whisker plot.

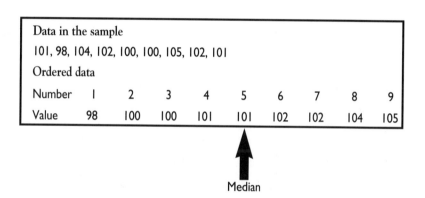

Data in the sample

101, 98, 104, 102, 100, 100, 105, 102, 101

Ordered data

Number	1	2	3	4	5	6	7	8	9
Value	98	100	100	101	101	102	102	104	105

Median

Figure 4.14
Marking of the median in the data of Figure 4.13.

Find the number that is just above one fourth of the numbers in the sample. In this case it is 100. It is called the *lower quartile* and it has the symbol Q1. It forms the lower end of the box (Figure 4.15).

Find the number that has 3/4 of the numbers less than it is. In this case it is 103. This is called the *upper quartile*. It has a symbol of Q3. It forms the upper end of the box (Figure 4.16).

Find the lowest and highest data values and draw the whisker lines on the box.

Another example of a box-and-whisker plot is shown in Figure 4.17.

Variability of day 2 is greater but not excessive. Average does not vary significantly from day to day.

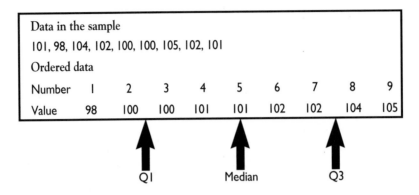

Figure 4.15
Marking of the first and third quartiles
for data of Figure 4.13.

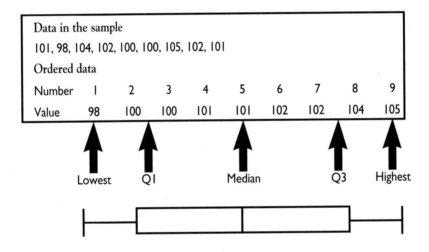

Figure 4.16
Marking of the lowest and highest values for the data of
Figure 4.13 and the drawing of the box-and-whisker plot.

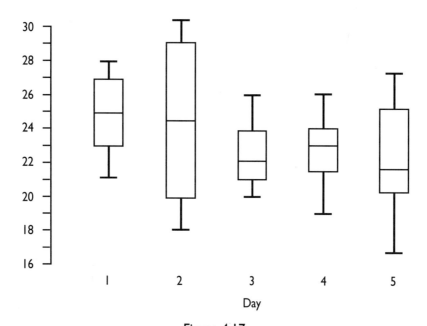

Figure 4.17
Box-and-whisker diagram for flow rates of a liquid
for valves manufactured on five different days.

REGRESSION ANALYSIS

In the scatter diagram, we see that the data of two variables plotted against each other can show whether the variables are related. This is done by looking at the plot and deciding if there is enough evidence to support the conclusion. A straight line or a curved line is often used to help us. It can show *how* the variables *might be* related. We are talking about variables that are related mathematically, so we must be careful. They are not always cause-and-effect relations. A person once told me that he could predict the stock market using the height of Lake Superior. For 30 years the two had followed each other up and down. He did not last long in the stock market. The height of Lake Superior did not cause the market to go up or down.

Many things are caused by something else acting on them. For example:
- The yield of a chemical process is affected by temperature.
- Mileage is affected by how fast we drive.
- The weight of paper is affected by its thickness.

Figure 4.18 shows a scatter diagram with a line drawn by a computer.

The computer will give us two numbers for the straight line. These are the *intercept* and the *slope*. The intercept is the value of variable plotted on the vertical line when the other variable is zero. The slope is the amount of pitch of the line. It is the vertical rise for a given horizontal distance.

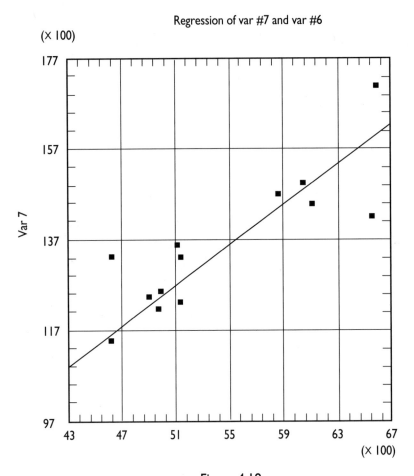

Regression of var #7 and var #6

Figure 4.18
Regression line calculated by computer and drawn on a scatter
diagram of the relationship between variables numbers 6 and 7
of a recent experiment on plastic sheeting.

ADDITIONAL INFORMATION ON REGRESSION ANALYSIS

In the scatter diagram, we see that the data of two variables plotted against each other can show whether the variables are related. A straight line or a curved line is used to show how they may be related. We put the data from the scatter diagram into a computer or calculator. The right buttons are pushed and a *regression line* is defined for us. What we get depends on the type of computer. Some call them a and b, while others call them b_0 and b_1.

$$a = b_0 = \text{the intercept}$$
$$b = b_1 = \text{the slope}$$

One variable is plotted on the vertical axis and is called y. This is the *dependent* variable (Figure 4.19). Its value depends on the value of the other variable. It usually is what is measured as a result of the process. Yield, gas mileage, or paper weight are examples of dependent variables.

The other variable is plotted on the horizontal axis and is called x. This is the *independent* variable (Figure 4.19). It usually is what is controlled in the process. Temperature, speed, or paper thickness are examples of independent variables. The form of the line is:

$$y = b_0 + b_1 (x)$$

The most important thing is that the computer can plot the data and the line for you. If it does, *look at the line!* If the data and the line go together then it is called a good *fit*. Often the data and the line do not go together, as seen in Figure 4.20. In these cases you should not use the regression line. Get a statistician or quality engineer to help you.

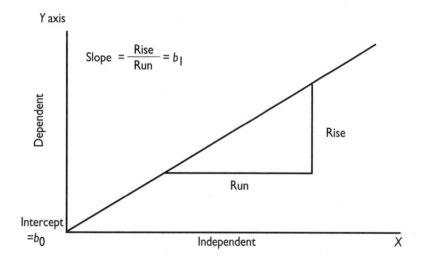

Figure 4.19
General regression line plotted to show the various definitions
of the components of a regression plot.

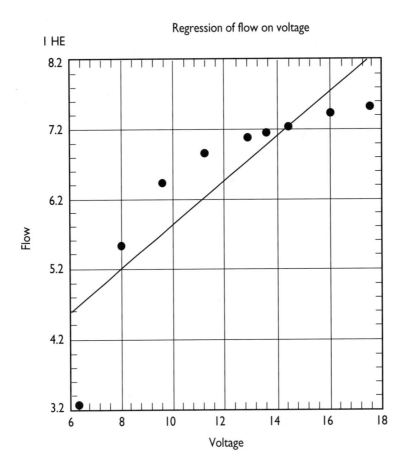

Figure 4.20
Regression line calculated by computer and drawn
on the scatter diagram of Figure 3.13.

CONTROL CHARTS

Control charts are trend charts with several lines added to help you decide whether or not you have a problem (Figure 4.21). Samples are taken from the process and plotted on the charts while the process is running. There are several key parts of control charts:

1. There is always a time or sequence scale.

2. There usually are two charts, one for averages and one for variability (range).

3. There is a center line which is the average of all the data.

4. There are two *control limit* lines for each chart. The control limit lines are calculated by computer or a quality specialist.

Using these lines it is easier to determine when you have a problem. As long as the plotted points stay inside the control limit lines, the process is acting naturally. There is no need to change anything. This goes for both average and range charts. A plotted point outside of the limits tells us that the process has changed. We should take some action. Most companies now are writing corrective action guidelines to tell operators what to do.

Sometimes, however, we can see some changes even if the plotted points are inside the control limit lines. They are the same types of changes that we saw in the trend plots. These are runs above or below the average, trends up or down, alternating patterns, and cycles. These are shown in Figure 4.22.

If you notice something unusual on the chart, you should take action. Call a supervisor or quality specialist.

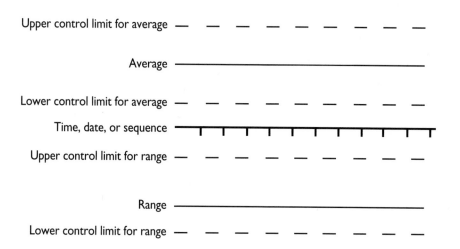

Figure 4.21
Components of a control chart.

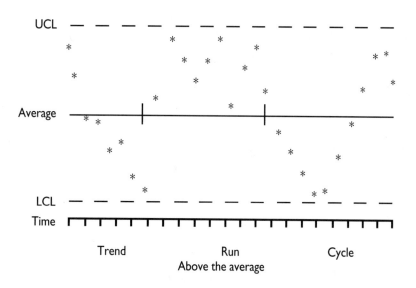

Figure 4.22
Example of a trend, run, and cycle applied to a control chart.

ADDITIONAL INFORMATION ON CONTROL CHARTS

The most common control chart for measured values is the Shewhart chart. This chart is named for Walter A. Shewhart, who invented the control chart. It is started by taking a regular sample of two or more pieces from a continuous production line. This can be done on a time basis such as one sample of four pieces every 15 minutes. It also can be done on a piece-rate basis such as on a sample of four pieces after every 100 pieces are made. An average and a range are calculated for each sample. Inexpensive hand calculators can greatly simplify this process. Most companies provide a recording and calculating sheet like the one shown in Figure 4.23.

After we have obtained 12 or more samples, we can plot a control chart. This is called a *stage I control chart*. It is based on historical or past data. The stage I control chart is made in the following manner:

1. Add up all the separate ranges and divide by the number of samples that you have. This gives you the average range. This is often called *R-bar* (R with one bar over it, $\bar{R}$). This is also called the *center line* for the control chart of ranges.

2. Add up all the separate sample averages and divide by the number of samples. This gives you the *grand average*, usually called *X-double bar* (X with two bars over it, $\bar{\bar{X}}$). This also is called the center line for the control chart on averages.

3. Calculate the control limits using the formulas listed in Figure 4.24.

4. Plot the control chart. The chart of averages usually is plotted above the time, date, or sequence line. The chart of ranges usually is plotted below the time line.

5. Add the points for the averages and the ranges found for each sample. Draw lines between each average and the next one. Do the same for the ranges.

6. The control chart should look similar to the chart shown in Figure 4.25.

NOTE: The range chart should always be read first. If there is no change in the range, look at the average chart. If the range is out of control, fix that problem before trying to adjust the average.

Always remember to include the time, date, or sequence line on the chart. If it is not there, we cannot tell when something happened. Always remember to use dashed lines for the control limits and filled lines for the center lines.

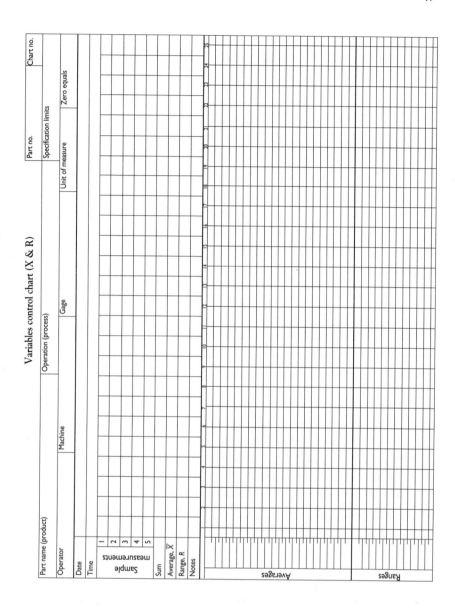

Figure 4.23
Example of a plotting and worksheet for control charts.

Sample size	Factors for			Formulas for computing control limits	
	Averages	Range		For Averages	For Range
n	A_2	D_3	D_4	$UCL_{\bar{X}} = \bar{\bar{X}} + A_2\bar{R}$	$UCL_R = D_4\bar{R}$
2	1.880	.0	3.268		
3	1.023	.0	2.574	$LCL_{\bar{X}} = \bar{\bar{X}} + A_2\bar{R}$	$LCL_R = D_3\bar{R}$
4	.729	.0	2.282		
5	.577	.0	2.114		
6	.483	.0	2.004		
7	.419	.076	1.924		
8	.373	.136	1.864		
9	.337	.184	1.816		
10	.308	.223	1.777		

Figure 4.24
Factors and equations for calculating the control
limits for X-bar and range control charts.

Look at the range chart that we created in Figure 4.25. All of the points are inside the control limits, and there are no patterns of the data like those we saw earlier. The range chart is *in control.*

Look at the average chart in Figure 4.25. There is one point outside of the control limits. The average control chart is *out of control.* We must find out what caused this point to be outside the limits. Once this is found, we must eliminate the cause. If we do not do this, it is likely to happen again and again. This is why we need to use corrective action guidelines.

After we have eliminated the cause of the sample being out of control, we drop these sample values and recalculate the center lines and limits. We are now ready to do a *stage II control chart.* This uses the stage I control chart that we have just completed. We now go into the process and take a sample at the regular time to do so. We calculate the average and the range as we did before and plot them right after the last point on each control chart (Figure 4.26).

If the points are inside the limits and do not show any trend, no action is taken on the process. It is in control. If the points are outside of the limits or there appears to be a trend, run, or cycle, we take action. This action should be in the corrective action guidelines or instructions from a supervisor.

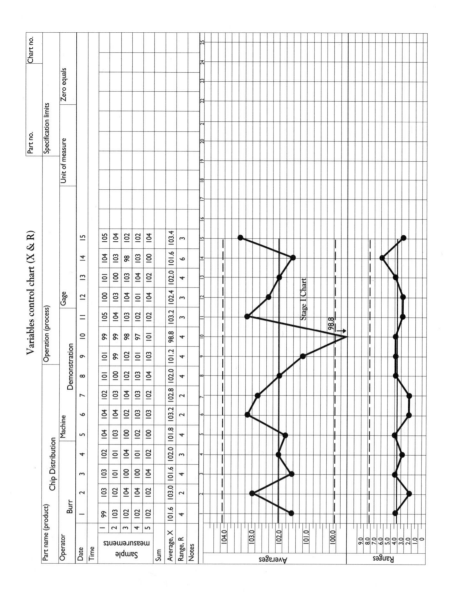

Figure 4.25
Stage I control chart generated by sampling the chip
distribution having an average life of 102.

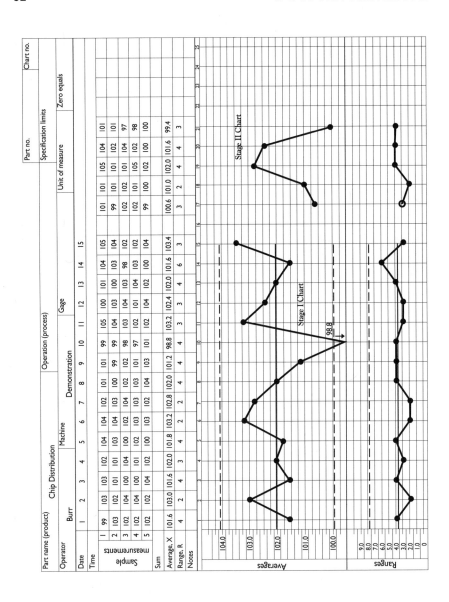

Figure 4.26
Continuation of the control chart (stage II) by sampling from the
chip distribution having an average of 100.

• •

CONFORMANCE CHARTS

Like the control chart, the conformance chart uses samples taken from the process. The conformance chart compares the average and the range of these samples to limits. These limits are based on tolerances and are called *conformance limits*.

The conformance limits are made very easily:

Center line = Nominal

Conformance limits = Nominal + (2/3) Half-tolerance

Example:

Specifications are 140 ± 3

Center line is 140

Conformance limits are 140 ± (2/3) Half-tolerance

140 ± (2/3) 3.0

140 ± 2.0

The plot of the sample data is similar to box-and-whisker plots, but does not have a box. They are made by a mark for the average and a line that represents the range (Figure 4.27).

If a line extends beyond the conformance limits, we are warned that the process may not be meeting specifications. If two lines in succession extend beyond the limits, we can be sure that the process is not meeting the specifications (Figure 4.28).

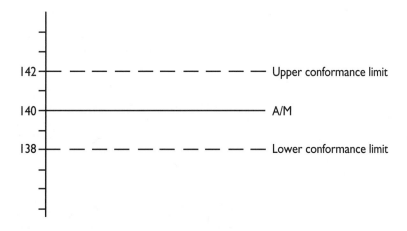

Figure 4.27

Plot of the conformance limits calculated for the rheostat knob data.

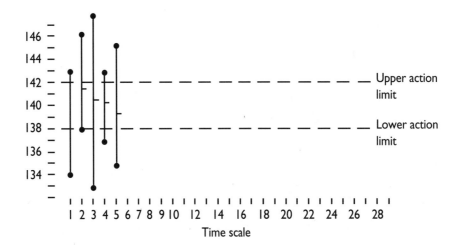

Figure 4.28
Plot of five samples of the rheostat data on the conformance chart.

ATTRIBUTES

Attributes are traits that make you, a machine, a part, or a job different from another like it. The shape of your nose, the color of your eyes, the shade of your hair, your height, your weight, your moles, and your scars are all attributes. A machine's downtime, its operating temperature, and its performance are attributes. A part has length, width, finish, defects, and imperfections. These are attributes. A job can be finished on time. It can be done right the first time, and it can be the right job. These also are attributes.

Attributes can be good or bad. Your nose may be too long or too short. You may have a small scar on your finger or a large birthmark on your cheek. The temperature of the machine may be too high. The part may have one defect which makes it unfit for use or only a few imperfections. The job may have to be done several times to get it right. These are examples of bad attributes. They are often called *nonconforming* because we do not want them. They do not conform to our quality goals. We use the word nonconforming instead of defective for legal reasons. In court, defects are those attributes that make the product unfit for use. Often we need to identify attributes that do not make the product unfit for use, and we call these nonconforming. A mole on my nose is a nonconforming attribute, but it does not make me defective!

In SPC, attributes are those things that we say are good/bad or go/no-go, or are the counted number of nonconforming things on the product.

In our toast example, burnt toast is bad. It is not fit for use and does not meet the specification of the customer. Let us say that we make toast once a day for 30 days and three pieces are burnt. This means that three divided by 30 is the average number of pieces burnt each day. Multiply this by 100 and we get the *percent nonconforming* pieces in the sample of 30 days. In this case, the process is making 10 percent nonconforming toast.

There are other attributes of toast that might make it unfit for use. One of these is holes. I do not like to eat toast that has a lot of holes in it. Melted butter goes through the holes and gets all over my fingers. It might even drip on the floor. I would like my toast with no holes but I am willing to eat toast with only two or fewer. Now I can count the holes in my toast that I made. This attribute is called the *number of nonconformities per sample*. It also means that each piece of toast had 40/30 = 1.3 holes on the average. This is called the *number of nonconformities per unit*.

On the average I did not make any bad pieces of toast during the 30 days. It is possible that one piece of toast did have more than two holes. And that piece does not meet my specification. It becomes a nonconforming piece of toast. It is unfit for use because it has too many holes.

- The number of nonconforming units in the sample is called d.
- The percent of nonconforming units in the sample is called $\%p$.
- The number of nonconformities in a sample is called c.
- The number of nonconformities per unit is called u.

ATTRIBUTE CONTROL CHARTS

We can make time plots and control charts for attributes just as we did for measurements.

For example, we can plot the number of nonconforming units that has been made each day. In this plot we assume that the production rate does not change very much at all. We could use this type of plot for the number of nonconforming units found in a sample taken each day. This is called a d-chart (Figure 4.29).

We also could plot the percent of nonconforming units that has been made each day. This is a very useful plot when the production rate changes quite a bit from day to day. That is why the control limits change from time to time. This is called a $\%p$-chart (Figure 4.30).

We can plot the number of nonconformities or imperfections on a sample of units produced each day. We also could plot the number of nonconformities on all the units produced each day if we inspect all of them. This is called a c-chart (Figure 4.31).

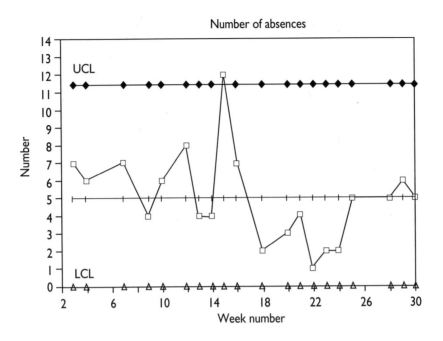

Figure 4.29
d-chart for the number of absences in a department.

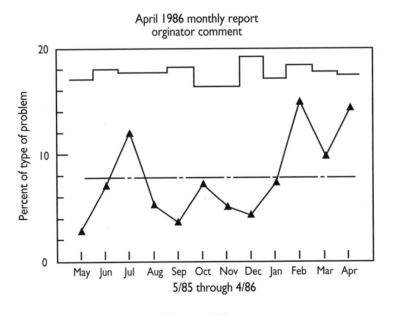

Figure 4.30
%*p*-chart for one cause of customer problems. The upper limit
varies because the number of experiments varies each month.

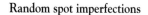

Random spot imperfections

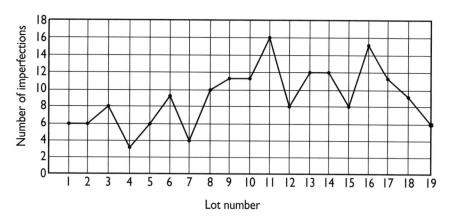

Lot number

Figure 4.31
c-chart for random spot imperfections on a sheet of plastic material.

We also can plot the average number of nonconformities per unit for each day. This plot is useful when the number of units produced each day varies quite a bit. This plot also can be used when we are counting the number of nonconformities per unit area. An example of this might be spots per square foot on plastic film. This is called a *u*-chart (Figure 4.32).

There are other attribute charts that can be made and used. They are similar to the ones described here and are read the same way. Attribute control charts are read in the same manner as control charts for measurements. Any points that are beyond the control limits are out of control. Trends going up or down, runs above or below average, and cycles also indicate out-of-control processes.

NOTE: It is important to discover when the process improves. This is seen by a run below the average or a trend down. We need to know this so that we can keep doing whatever it is that has improved the process. Improvement might be seen when we use better raw materials or have done a better job of training the operator.

If there is evidence that the process has changed, corrective action guidelines should be available to tell you what to do. If you do not have these, then you should notify your supervisor.

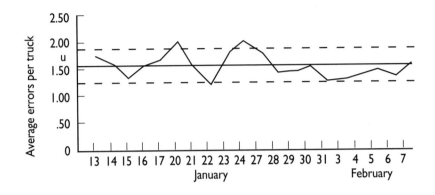

Figure 4.32
u-chart for the average errors per truck for 20 days of production.

ADDITIONAL INFORMATION ABOUT ATTRIBUTE CONTROL CHARTS

d-chart—Samples of the same number of units are taken in some manner to represent the product made. These samples can be from the production of a day, shift, hour, or any other time desired. The samples are usually taken from a single machine or a work center. The samples must be the same size or very nearly the same size (Figure 4.33).

%*p*-chart—Samples are taken to represent the production of some time period. This can be for a week, day, shift, hour, or other time period. Usually the samples are taken from a single machine or work center. Very often all the units made are inspected and judged to be good or bad. This means that the sample size is all of the units produced during the test time period. This also means that the sample size will vary greatly. Use a %*p*-chart when the sample size varies (Figure 4.34).

c-chart—Samples are taken and the number of nonconformities are counted in all of the units that make up the sample. There may be more than one nonconformity on any one unit. The nonconformities may be the same or different types. The units may or may not be defective because of the nonconformities. In using a *c*-chart, we do not count the number of defective units. The sample size must be the same or very nearly the same if we want to use a *c*-chart (Figure 4.35).

d = Number of nonconforming units

$\overline{n}$ = Sample size

$$\frac{\Sigma d}{\Sigma n} = \overline{d} \qquad\qquad \overline{p} = \frac{\overline{d}}{\overline{n}}$$

$$s_d = \sqrt{n\overline{p}(1 - \overline{p})} = \sqrt{\overline{d}(1 - \overline{p})}$$

Center line = $\overline{d}$

Control limits = $\overline{d} \pm 3s_d$

Figure 4.33
Calculations for the control limits for a d-chart.

$$\%p = \frac{d}{n} \times 100$$

$$\%p = \frac{\Sigma d}{\Sigma n} \times 100$$

$$s\,\%p = \sqrt{\frac{\overline{\%p}(100 - \overline{\%p})}{n}}$$

Center line = $\overline{\%p}$

Control limits = $\overline{\%p} \pm 3s\%p$

Figure 4.34
Calculations for the control limits for a $\%p$-chart.

c = Number of nonconformities in sample of n units

k = Number of samples of size n taken

$$\bar{c} = \frac{\Sigma c}{k}$$

$$s_c = \sqrt{\bar{c}}$$

Center line = $\bar{c}$

Control limits = $\bar{c} \pm 3s_c$

Figure 4.35
Calculations for the control limits for a c-chart.

u-chart—As in the c-chart, the number of nonconformities is counted for a sample of units. The nonconformities may be the same or different types. There may be one or more nonconformities for any one unit. The unit may or may not be defective because of the nonconformities. In making a u-chart, we do not count the number of defective units. The sample size may vary and can include all the units produced during the time period (Figure 4.36).

u = Nonconformities per unit

n = Sample size

$$u = \frac{c}{n}$$

$$\bar{u} = \frac{\Sigma c}{\Sigma n}$$

$$s_u = \sqrt{\frac{\bar{u}}{n}}$$

Center line = $\bar{u}$

Control limits = $\bar{u} \pm 3s_u$

Figure 4.36
Calculations for the control limits of a u-chart.

5
PUTTING THE TOOLS TOGETHER

· ·

Before anything can happen in your company, the managers must lead the effort. This also is true for starting and using SPC. The SPC effort must be part of an overall *total quality program*. The managers must plan for quality and they must know what it is all about. The managers cannot just talk about it; they must lead the effort. This means all managers, from the president to the first line supervisors.

The first thing that is needed to start using these tools is a team. This team can be called together to solve problems or to begin SPC on a process. The members of the team should include anyone who can help the team meet its objective. The people who work as a part of the process must be on the team. They know more about the process than anyone else. Management will need to select a team and let the team know what is expected of it. The team should be made up of five to eight people. These could include operators, first line supervisors, engineers, maintenance technicians, and quality assurance specialists. The team must be trained in the use of the tools. The team's efforts must be reviewed by management regularly. The team's suggestions and requests must be acted on. If management cannot act on a request or suggestion, it must let the team know why it cannot. The team's success must be recognized and celebrated by management.

Figure 5.1 shows a flow diagram of one way to implement SPC by the team.

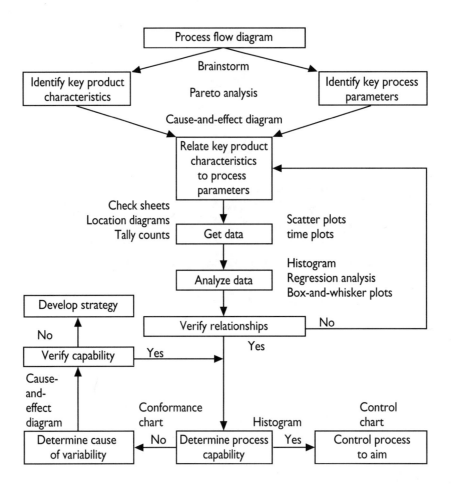

Figure 5.1
Flow diagram for the implementation of SPC.

Appendix
INSTRUCTOR'S GUIDE
••••••••••••••••••••••••••••••

USING THIS BOOK FOR INSTRUCTION

This manual has been written in a modular style. Each tool has textual material in one or more levels. Each level builds on the preceding one(s). Instructors can select the level(s) most appropriate to the application in their company. This manual is constructed so that instructors can select the tool(s) most appropriate to their company and application.

In any training program, and this one specifically, it is necessary to gain the visible support of top management. This is best demonstrated by the actual participation of top management in the training. While it is preferable that they attend all the sessions, this usually is not feasible.

Recommendation: At the very least, top management should give a presentation at the start of the first session of the program to set the tone of the training program and be available to answer questions then and at the end of the program.

I have found that when the SPC tools are introduced into the unit for the first time, there is a great chance that too much information will be given to the student. This likely will result in the overloading of the mind and little application of the tools.

Recommendation: Do not introduce more than the first three tools in the first session(s). Provide practice in class and require that homework be done between sessions.

I also have found that while set examples to be worked out in class may be all right, real-life applications from the participants current work are much better.

Recommendation: Use real, current examples of processes, problems, goals, and data indigenous to the participants' work areas.

The best use of these tools and the highest success rate of application of these tools will come when there are natural work groups or assigned task teams taking the program together. These work groups or teams need to have clearly defined objectives and charges from their supervision before they go to class.

Recommendation: Train in rational subgroups whenever possible and hold the groups accountable for applying what they learn to their problem, objective, or charge.

POSSIBLE COURSE OUTLINES

INTRODUCTION TO QUALITY AND THE USE OF SPC TOOLS

Four modules totaling about 12 to 16 hours have been designed for a basic introduction to the SPC tools. These could be presented in two- or four-hour sessions as appropriate.

Objectives: To provide the participants with (1) an understanding of the need for quality improvement, (2) why and how the SPC tools are used to communicate with each other and management, and (3) an introduction on how to solve problems using these tools.

Module	Subject material
1	Introduction by top manager
	What is quality?
	Need for quality improvement
	Process vs. product control—burnt toast
	Class creates flow and cause-and-effect diagrams for toast
	Select most likely cause(s)—Pareto analysis
	Participants identify process or problem for next class
2	Review of homework—project selection
	Visualizing your process—flow diagrams
	Identifying problems and causes—cause-and-effect diagrams
	Selecting what to work on—Pareto analysis
	Collecting data—what to measure
	Specifications and tolerances
	Visualizing data—getting data on toast
	Participants make a flow, cause-and-effect, or Pareto diagram
3	Review of homework
	Visualizing data
	• Histograms
	• Process capability
	• Scatter diagrams
	• Trend plots
	• Control charts
	Participants make a histogram, scatter diagram, or trend plot for next class

4   Review of homework
           Continuing visualizing data tools
           Putting the tools together
           Identifying opportunities for quality improvement

Five modules totaling about 16 to 20 hours have been designed for teaching the use of SPC tools. These could be presented in two- or four-hour sessions as appropriate.

Objectives: To provide the participants with (1) an understanding of how the SPC tools are constructed and used for quality improvements, (2) methods of handling and analyzing information and data, and (3) a process they can incorporate in their work every day.

Module	*Subject material*
1	Visualizing information

           • Making and using process flow diagrams
           • Brainstorming techniques
           • Making and using cause-and-effect diagrams
           • Making decisions using Pareto analysis and voting
           • Workshops with subgroups on each tool

2   Visualizing data
           • Finding something to measure
           • Collecting data and making it visible
               – Check sheets
               – Location diagrams
               – Tally counts
               – Time plots
               – Scatter diagrams

3   Making and using histograms
           • Exercises in constructing histograms
           • Process capability and measures of compatibility
           • Exercises in calculating the capability

4   Making and using control charts for measurements
           • Construction of limits (if appropriate)
           • Reading the control chart
           • What to do when the process is out of control

5   Making and using control charts for attributes
           • What are attributes?
           • Uses of attribute control charts
           • Examples of attribute control charts
           • Reaching attribute control charts

MAKING CHIP DISTRIBUTIONS FOR DEMONSTRATIONS AND EXERCISES

Chip distributions are very effective in demonstrating how samples are taken from a process, in showing the effect of sample size, in demonstrating the construction of histograms and control charts, and in explaining process capability. There are chip distributions available commercially; however, they tend to be relatively expensive. The quincunx also is a very effective tool for demonstrating these principles, but it can cost as much as $800.

For a few dollars and the expenditure of an evening, your own chip distributions can be made easily. You will need the following materials:

- A red and blue permanent marker pen (other colors also may be useful)
- Several packages of metal-rimmed paperboard key tags
- Several small opaque plastic food storage boxes

Using Figure A.1, choose a distribution and arrange 200 tags in piles according to the frequency table.

Mark the appropriate numbers on the tags with either the red or blue pen. Place in a box and sample the tags as needed. You can take as many as 10 or so

Approximately normal populations for sampling experiments

Number x	A	B	C	D	E	F	G
+ 11				1			
+ 10			1	1			
+ 9			1	1	1		
+ 8			1	3	3		
+ 7		1	3	5	10		
+ 6		3	5	8	23		
+ 5	1	10	8	12	39		
+ 4	3	23	12	16	48		
+ 3	10	39	16	20	39	1	
+ 2	23	48	20	22	23	3	
+ 1	39	39	22	23	10	10	1
0	48	23	23	22	3	23	3
- 1	39	10	22	20	1	39	10
- 2	23	3	20	16		48	23
- 3	10	1	16	12		39	39
- 4	3		12	8		23	48
- 5	1		8	5		10	39
- 6			5	3		3	23
- 7			3	1		1	10
- 8			1	1			3
- 9			1	1			1
- 10			1				
N	200	200	201	201	200	200	200
μ	0	+ 2	+ 0	+ 1	+ 4	- 2	- 4
σX	1.715	1.715	3.47	3.47	1.715	1.715	1.715

Figure A.1
Frequency tables for the generation of chip distributions.

tags from the distribution without affecting the probabilities of the sampling. It usually is a good idea to count the tags after a demonstration to ensure the integrity of the distribution.

A second distribution can be placed on the reverse side of the tags. Randomly mix the tags face down. Arrange the tags in piles according to the second distribution and mark the tags accordingly with a pen having a different color than the opposite side.

I have used the A and B distributions effectively for most SPC demonstrations.

For the simulation of making toast, I have created a distribution of color (brown ink) and on the opposite side, age of the bread (orange ink). The distributions are given in the next section. This distribution has 60 tags and should only be sampled singly with replacement. This arrangement allows the demonstrator to collect data on the color and the age simultaneously. Once the data are collected, tally counts, trend plots, and a scatter diagram can be made.

SUGGESTED CLASS EXERCISES

MAKING TOAST

The author's favorite exercise to introduce the tools of SPC is the making of toast. This exercise was originally developed by Al Rickmers and has been extended by both he and the author in many different directions as the audience/class makeup dictates.

Materials

Overhead transparencies and pens (preferred) or newsprint and pens; chip distribution—See Figure A.2.

Exercise 1

Draw or have drawn a picture of a toaster.

SPC is similar to what happens when using a toaster. When you get up in the morning, you put bread into the toaster. You press down on the lever and later the toasted bread pops up. If the toast is burnt, you have a choice. You can scrape the black off and eat the result. This makes the toast edible, but what will happen the next time you make toast? Of course, the next batch will burn, too. And the next and the next. This is *product control*.

Product control sorts out the bad product from the good product so that the good product can be sold and the bad product can be reworked or thrown away. For the process of toasting bread, you can do something about the process. You can change the setting on the side of the toaster to make lighter toast the next time. This is your other choice when the toast burns. You have just performed *process control*.

NOTE: During the conduct of these exercises do not name the SPC tool being used at the time.

Number on the tag

Brown distribution	Orange distribution
2	4
3	4 ea 5
3	6
4	2 ea 5
4	22 ea 6
4	7
5	4 ea 6
5	22 ea 7
5	1 ea 8
6	2 ea 7
6	11 ea 8
6	2 ea 9
7	3 ea 8
7	2 ea 9
8	9

Frequency distributions

Number	Brown frequency	Orange frequency
1		
2	1	
3	5	
4	15	1
5	27	6
6	16	17
7	5	25
8	1	15
9		5

Brown average = 5.0
Brown standard deviation = 1.1

Orange average = 6.9
Orange standard deviation = 1.1

Figure A.2

Distribution for demonstrating making toast.

Exercise 2

Develop a process flow diagram on making toast. Use the usual techniques to do this. Ask yourself, what is the first thing? What is the next? And so on. The result should look something like Figure 1.1. Ask for actions when toast is not satisfactory. You should receive answers such as:

- Scrape it—rework.
- Throw it out—scrap.
- Give it to the dog—reviewed release.
- Eat it anyway.

Exercise 3

Develop a cause-and-effect diagram for making good toast or for a problem with burnt toast. It should look something like Figure 1.6.

Exercise 4

Have the participants vote for the *major branch* of the cause-and-effect diagram that is most likely to have the greatest effect on the quality of the toast. Count the votes for each of the branches and place them on the diagram. (Usually they split between the operator and the toaster.) I often ask each side to explain its position. This usually results in the operator/group persuading the others that the operator controls the process by observation and adjustment.

Exercise 5

Put up the flow diagram. Have the participants identify any measurements that could be made on the product, process, or starting material. Without too much prompting, they usually identify the characteristics of the bread that are on the cause-and-effect diagram, time of waiting, and several characteristics of the toast (e.g., hardness, color, etc.). Note these on the flow diagram.

Exercise 6

Ask the class members how they might specify color of the product. They may suggest "brown," "light brown," or "medium," etc. Either they will suggest a numbering system, or you may suggest one. The system is to make nine pieces of toast having shades of color from very light (1) to burnt (9). Take a picture of the pieces or vacuum pack them in plastic to make a visual comparison chart. I usually introduce a set of specifications that are a nominal of five with tolerance limits of ±2.

Exercise 7

Have one of the participants draw samples five at a time from a chip distribution, Figure A.2, which has the color of the toast on one side and the age in days of the bread on the other. Record the data at the top of the newsprint or overhead material. I usually only record 20 chips to save time but 30 might be better. Record the color on the first line with the corresponding age directly below.

Exercise 8

Make a tally count of the toast color only. Place the specification limits on the tally count. Ask whether the toast is in or out of specifications. Often the samples will all be in spec. Next, ask whether all toast ever made from the distribution will be in spec. Then draw the smooth curve over the tally count to show the tails out of spec.

Tally counts are to compare data to tolerances.

Exercise 9

Make a run chart of the color data only. Draw a line between the points. Ask whether there was any change in the process during the making of the toast. (I never have observed one.)

Run charts demonstrate whether the process has changed.

Exercise 10

Make a scatter diagram of the data of the color and age of the bread. Ask if there is a relationship between the bread's color and age. The answer will be that it is obvious.

Scatter diagrams demonstrate whether there are relationships between one thing and another.

Summarize the toast exercise by pointing out that if we can do all this with making toast we can do it with anything whether it is in the office or on the manufacturing floor.

NOTE: I have extended this series of exercises to the delivery of services (e.g., distribution houses, by introducing a waitress to deliver the toast to the customer). The roles of the cook, waitress, and customer lead to some lively discussions. Mr. Rickmers and I also have introduced concept of process capability (without use of statistics) and reduction of variability.

Exercise of reduction of toast variability

Ask the participants for ways to control variability using the flow and cause-and-effect diagrams. Again use voting to establish a priority for implementation. Pick an effect and simulate a new toast distribution by using another chip distribution (not very efficient) or use an overhead transparency with the following color values:

   6,6,5,5,4   5,5,6,4,5   5,5,5,6,5   4,5,5,5,5

Compare the tally count of this to that of the original toast. Now pick another one or two effects on variability and simulate a third toast distribution on another transparency with the following color values:

   5,5,5,5,4   5,5,5,6,5   4,5,5,5,5   4,5,5,5,5

Again compare the three tally counts.

USING THE NORMAL CHIP DISTRIBUTIONS

The author has effectively used the A (red) and B (blue) distributions (Figure A.1) for most SPC demonstrations. One way to accomplish this is to use the distribution as if it were a machine.

Exercise 1

Here is the machine (chips in a box). What do we do now to make product? Eventually the group will identify the following:

a. Need for operator—assign one.

b. Training for the operator—show operator how to take sample and add 100 to number on the chip; show only blue distribution, but do not specify color.

c. Need for tolerances—102 ± 4.

d. First-piece inspection.

e. Need for first four to five pieces to be within middle 50 percent of specification.

f. Need for about 40 pieces to determine what the machine is capable of producing under these best conditions.

Exercise 2

Select three more pieces (after the first-piece inspection); if they are not all within the middle 50 percent of the specs, retrain the operator (the operator may have read the red color).

NOTE: Since this distribution is *not* capable of meeting the specifications, it may require several tries. I have admonished the operator to work harder and think, and occasionally have changed operators.

Record the chip values on the tally count and by groups of five on another chart board or overhead. Select eight groups of five each filling out the tally count as you progress.

Exercise 3

Compare tally count to the tolerances. Estimate the variability by dividing the overall *range* by five (for samples of approximately 30 to 80). Six times this number will give a fair estimate of the machine's capability. Compare this figure to the tolerances. In almost all cases the tolerances are smaller than the distribution spread.

The instructor may want to introduce C_p and C_{pk} at this point in the discussion.

After introducing the concepts of process control and control charts the following exercises can be performed.

Exercise 4

Using the grouped data (by fives), calculate the average and range of each group. Calculate the average of the averages and the average range. From these figures, calculate the control limits for the average and range charts. This is called a *stage I* control chart (i.e., made from historical data).

Exercise 5

Using the chip distribution, select several groups of five from the blue distribution and plot the results on the control chart making the decision to continue or stop after each plot (*stage II*). Ask the operator to switch to the red distribution and proceed until the class tells you to stop (i.e., a change has been noted).

NOTE: It also is effective if the operator is told privately to make the switch without telling anyone.

THE WHALE ANALOGY TO PROCESS CONTROL

The following is a possible script for an analogy that I found helpful in communicating the concepts of process control. At first it may appear silly, but it is exceedingly effective in its communication. This humble story is fun and will be remembered long after the techniques are forgotten. Although I have suggested a particular script, it always is better for the instructor to adapt it to his or her own style and locale.

• •

My mother-in-law (my parents or I) had Ralph and Sam as her next-door neighbors in Florida. One day when I was visiting, Sam came over and asked me how he could tell if his new swimming pool was exactly 3 feet deep. He needed to know this because his children are 3 feet 6 inches tall and any more water could cause them to drown since they do not know how to swim. I suggested that he get a yardstick, and if the water was more than 3 feet his fingers would get wet. He argued that he could not do this all the time as it rains in Florida. Was there any way to monitor the depth? I suggested that he get a marine depth finder and a strip chart recorder.
[Show the pool overhead (have card in place).]
  • Identify the depth finder in the cork ring.
  • Show the chart reading up to 3:00.
  • Ask:
        –What is the level of the water?
        –Is it always the same level?
        –What is causing the variation?

Sam was delighted. The other neighbor, Ralph, had a pet whale which he kept around the house. Now this whale became bored this day and decided to go for a walk. After strolling out about 20 blocks, over several blocks, the whale became very hot and sweaty so he decided to return home. On the way he passed Sam's house and saw, through the open gate, Sam's new swimming pool. It looked so inviting that the whale went for a swim.

Meanwhile, Sam, Ralph, and I were sipping a few martinis and were not paying much attention to what was happening. After a while, Ralph went home, found his pet whale gone and returned asking if we had seen it. I looked at the strip chart recorder.
[Show the recorder to 8:00.]
  Ask:
  • When did the whale go into the pool?
  • Did he slide in or jump in?
  • Is he still in the pool?
"No, I haven't seen your whale but I know where he is!" I answered.
  Ask:
  • Now what can be done?
  Some possible answers:
  • Drain the pool to 3 feet but what happens when the whale leaves? Add water to 3 feet. (Very expensive.)

How deep is the water?
(depth sounder)

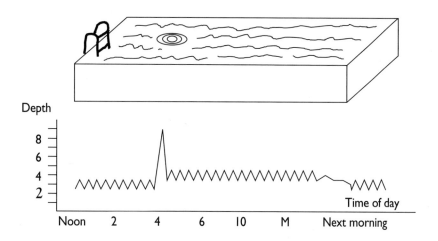

• Build a 5,000 gallon tank for overflow and add a pump to return water to the pool automatically when the whale leaves. Elegant engineering solution. $10,000 for $5,000 pool.

• Shoot the whale. Lose Ralph's friendship.

• Teach the kids to swim in 4 feet of water with the whale. (It's a killer whale.)

• Get the whale out of the pool.

We called AAA but it didn't arrive until the next morning. We pulled the whale out of the pool.

[Show the remainder of the chart.]

• Did it come out fast or slow?

• What is the level of the pool now? (Three feet unless he had a drink or left something behind.)

• Have we finished the task?

Finishing the task:

• Shoot the whale (lose Ralph as a friend).

• Cut the whale's legs off (encyclopedia reports that whales don't have legs).

• Lock the gate (kids can't get in or out).

• Make the gate narrower (Ralph can't get through—have you seen Ralph?).

• Shoot Ralph.

• Make Sam get his own swimming pool.

Eventually you will get it:
Put a spring and a lift latch on the gate (since the encyclopedia reports that whales cannot climb fences, it will work).

Now this is a ridiculous story, but it is used to show that any process has whales that can jump into or out of it. They can slide in or out. They can porpoise in and out. They can be big whales, little whales, or even little fish. They can be entire schools of fish or pods of whales.
[Show the various types of whales in processes.]

Trends, shifts, cycles.

Show some real examples of whales in processes.

NOTE: This humble story is fun and will be remembered long after the techniques are forgotten. The moral of the tale is: Get the whales out of your processes!

MORE SUGGESTED CLASS EXERCISES

It always is best to practice the tools on real problems that are important to the participants. The instructor should strive to identify problems in the unit(s) undergoing training. The instructor should also strive to obtain data from the unit prior to classes and apply tools to the data. One way to do this is to have participants bring in homework with data or problems.

If the participants have diverse backgrounds, position levels, and job descriptions, the instructor may want to use the suggestions that follow or think up some others.

Exercises for process flow diagrams
- Telephone tag
- Going fishing
- Delivering goods
- Getting admitted to a hospital

Exercises for cause-and-effect diagrams
- Getting to work on time
- Cleaning the house
- Mowing the lawn
- Holding a disastrous meeting

Exercise for Pareto analysis

Give each person five votes and have them spread them out over a cause-and-effect diagram. They can put any number of votes (up to five) on any single cause or on five different causes. Tally up and arrange the votes in a Pareto diagram.

Exercises for finding things to measure

What could you measure of a service being provided you by one of the following:

- Window washer
- Custodian
- Medical treatment
- Payroll

These exercises can be done by the entire class or the class can be broken up into subgroups.

SELECTED READINGS

· ·

(References are listed in order of increasing difficulty and use of statistics.)

Ishikawa, Kaoru. *Guide to Quality Control.* Tokyo: Asian Productivity Organization, 1982.

ASQC Automotive Division. *Statistical Process Control Manual.* Milwaukee: American Society for Quality Control, 1986.

Kern, Jill P., Riley, John J., and Jones, Louis N. *Human Resources Management.* Milwaukee: ASQC Quality Press, 1987.

Burr, Irving W. *Elementary Statistical Quality Control.* New York: Marcel Dekker, 1979.

INDEX